The Handbook of Mascots & Nicknames

**A Guide to the Nicknames of all
Senior, Junior, and Community Colleges
throughout the United States and Canada**

Peter J. Fournier

The Handbook of Mascots & Nicknames
Copyright © 2003 Raja & Associates

ISBN: 0-9741136-0-3

Library of Congress Control Number: 2003093177

This book is intended as an educational and informational resource.
The publisher and author expressly disclaim any responsibility or liability in
connection with the use of this book.

Interior Design: Publishing Professionals, Port Richey, FL
Cover Design: Sara L. Gardner

Manufactured in the United States of America

Table of Contents

Preface

This book is the result of several years of research and investigation. It is intended as a resource for settling barroom arguments or for playing trivia games. I admit that, although I have included almost 1500 senior college entries, over 740 junior college entries, and over 115 Canadian college entries, the list is probably not complete. I would gladly like to hear from any officials, students, etc. of those institutions that I may have omitted, and their mascot or nickname will surely be included in the next revision of this book.

Each section of this book is divided into two subsections, i.e., a list of institutions in alphabetical order and a list of mascots or nicknames in alphabetical order. This reference is intended to supply the layman with a "quick and easy" reference for fun and games.

No attempt has been made to segregate the entries by division, conference, organization, etc. Not all of the institutions may field teams in all of the major sports. The only criteria were that the institutions compete intercollegiately in any sport, and that the athletic team has a nickname or mascot. I have also found that many ladies teams use the male nickname or mascot with the word "Lady" before it. Thus, I have only included the female nickname or mascot if it is very different from the male.

Pete Fournier
c/o Raja & Associates
16807 Harrierridge Place
Lithia, FL 33547

Out of Bounds
Don Allen

Black, White and Red All Over
Athletic nicknames produce thin skins and thicker heads.

If anyone doubts how obsessed we've become with political correctness in our culture, just head to the NCAA Web site and check out the story on collegiate nicknames. The NCAA, apparently with nothing better to do, have now determined that the universities and colleges under the organization's blanket of control need to do a better job of policing themselves when it comes to hurting other people's feelings.

The NCAA has always been big on matters of appearance rather than substance.

At the heart of the matter, of course, is the controversy concerning the use of Native American lore as nicknames and mascots. Perish the thought that the NCAA come right out and demand that Florida State drop its Seminole designation, or at least eliminate the guy in buckskin and war paint who plants a spear at mid-field before a football game. Forget the possibility that the organization tells the Arkansas State administration that those three fringed-up college kids parading around like Geronimo and his tribe at Indian athletic events is a practice deemed unacceptable. We've got a better chance of seeing the island of Manhattan returned to its original owners.

With the NCAA, it's often all about appearances. Sometimes you get the feeling that the governing body would rather be considered politically correct than effective. What with the alarming number of university athletic programs currently on probation, the even greater number of programs in serious financial straits and the highly debated question of a Division-1A football playoff system on its plate, you have to wonder why the organization would concentrate instead on an issue such as this.

Because it makes them look good? Sounds reasonable to me.

Goodness knows, there are sensitivity issues at work here. While I'm not the most humanity-related columnist in the world, neither am I the ignorant, Neanderthal-like WASP whose caricature adorns the T-shirts now being sold in large numbers by the Fighting Whites intramural team from the University of Northern Colorado. Exasperated by the mascot debate, this group of students (both Native American and non-Indian) have created a nickname and logo ("Everythang's gonna be all white") that derides ethnic stereotyping. Monies received from the sale of Fighting Whites paraphernalia goes toward the establishment of a scholarship fund for Native American students.

Should we, as the white majority, be offended? Are you kidding? You mean, we should protest vehemently as we renew our season tickets to Washington Redskins games? Maybe we could fire off a letter to our congressman about the same time we send that check to the UL-Monroe Indian foundation or the athletic fund of the Central Michigan Chippewas?

Issues of respect—and disrespect—have reached absurd levels athletically. If a batter homers and then stands at the plate to admire it, he's disrespecting the pitcher. If a pitcher throws high and tight to a batter, he's showing disrespect. If a football team runs up the score, they're disrespecting the opponent.

You want respect? Earn it. Make a better pitch, play better defense. Get better, period. Just because you got hammered doesn't mean you were disrespected. It means you weren't good enough. There's a difference.

Just as there's a difference between nicknames. Granted, most reasonably intelligent individuals would admit that there's nothing remotely respectful about the term Redskins. But winners write the history books, and just how much stroke does a conquered people have when it comes to respect, anyway? Still, Miami of Ohio saw the light a few years ago and changed to the Redhawks. But the NFL franchise in Washington—jeez, our nation's capital—has stubbornly refused for reasons adhered to only by morons and politicians.

How long do you think that franchise would last if they were the Blackskins?

Yes, there are issues of genuine respect where mascots, nicknames and Native Americans are concerned. But most Americans—regardless of race, color and creed—will have a hard time buying into the accusation of disrespect where most of these schools are concerned. By my count, there are 324 Division 1-A football and basketball teams in the NCAA. Of this number, there are 11 institutions that might be considered politically incorrect where Native Americans—and the NCAA—are concerned.

Florida State Seminoles. Arkansas State Indians. Louisiana-Monroe Indians. Utah Utes. Hawaii Warriors. Alcorn State Braves. Bradley Braves. Quinnipiac Braves. Central Michigan Chippewas. Illinois Fighting Illini. San Diego State Aztecs.

Since the Aztecs disappeared almost 400 years ago, we might want to pass on the California school. Take away that nickname and the only thing left of the culture are ruins. On the other hand, I would think the NCAA might eventually become curious as to how Texas Tech and Colgate came up with the nickname, Red Raiders.

Knowing the NCAA, maybe not.

Don Allen has been with *The Times of Acadiana* for 14 years. E-mail him at timesedit@timesofacadiana.com.

Reprinted with permission: Judy Johnson, Editor, *The Times of Acadiana*

Part 1

Senior Colleges and Universities

United States

Alphabetic Listing by Institution

Did you know. . .

mas·cot, n. a person, animal, or thing
supposed to bring good luck.

*Random House Dictionary
of the English Language*

that the Harvard Crimson athletic teams
are sometimes known as "Cantabs"?

*This is an abbreviated form of
Cantabrigian, a native of Cambridge.*

Senior Colleges and Universities—United States
Alphabetic Listing by Institution

Institution Name	Location	Nickname/Mascot

A

Institution Name	Location	Nickname/Mascot
Abilene Christian University	Abilene, TX	Wildcats
Adams State College	Alamosa, CO	Grizzlies
Adelphi University	Garden City, NY	Panthers
Adrian College	Adrian, MI	Bulldogs
Agnes Scott College (Women)	Atlanta/Decatur, GA	Scotties
Akron, University of	Akron, OH	Zips
Alabama, University of	Tuscaloosa, AL	Crimson Tide
Alabama–Birmingham, University of	Birmingham, AL	Blazers
Alabama–Huntsville, University of	Huntsville, AL	Chargers
Alabama A & M University	Normal, AL	Bulldogs
Alabama State University	Montgomery, AL	Hornets
Alaska–Anchorage, University of	Anchorage, AK	Seawolves
Alaska–Fairbanks, University of	Fairbanks, AK	Nanooks
Alaska Pacific University	Anchorage, AK	Pioneers
Albany College of Pharmacy	Albany, NY	Panthers
Albany State University	Albany, GA	Golden Rams
Albertson College of Idaho	Caldwell, ID	Coyotes
Albertus Magnus College	New Haven, CT	Falcons
Albion College	Albion, MI	Britons
Albright College	Reading, PA	Lions
Alcorn State University	Lorman, MS	Braves
Alderson-Broaddus College	Philippi, WV	Battlers
Alfred University	Alfred, NY	Saxons
Alice Lloyd College	Pippa Passes, KY	Eagles
Allegheny College	Meadville, PA	Gators
Allen University	Columbia, SC	Yellow Jackets
Alliant International University	San Diego, CA	Mountain Lions
Alma College	Alma, MI	Scots
Alvernia College	Reading, PA	Crusaders
Alverno College (Women)	Milwaukee, WI	Inferno
American Indian College	Phoenix, AZ	Warriors
American International College	Springfield, MA	Yellow Jackets
American University	Washington, DC	Eagles
Amherst College	Amherst, MA	Lord Jeffs
Anderson College	Anderson, SC	Trojans
Anderson University	Anderson, IN	Ravens
Andrews University	Berrien Springs, MI	Cardinals
Angelo State University	San Angelo, TX	Rams
Anna Maria College	Paxton, MA	AMcats
Appalachian Bible College	Bradley, WV	Warriors
Appalachian State University	Boone, NC	Mountaineers

Senior Colleges and Universities—United States
Alphabetic Listing by Institution

Institution Name	Location	Nickname/Mascot
Aquinas College	Grand Rapids, MI	Saints
Aquinas College	Nashville, TN	Cavaliers
Arcadia College (formerly Beaver)	Glenside, PA	Scarlet Knights
Arizona, University of	Tucson, AZ	Wildcats
Arizona State University	Tempe, AZ	Sun Devils
Arkansas, University of	Fayetteville, AR	Razorbacks
Arkansas–Little Rock, University of	Little Rock, AR	Trojans
Arkansas–Monticello, University of	Monticello, AR	Boll Weevils
Arkansas–Pine Bluff, University of	Pine Bluff, AR	Golden Lions
Arkansas Baptist College	Little Rock, AR	Buffaloes
Arkansas State University	Jonesboro, AR	Indians
Arkansas Technical University	Russellville, AR	Wonder Boys/Golden Suns
Arlington Baptist College	Arlington, TX	Patriots
Armstrong Atlantic State University	Savannah, GA	Pirates
Asbury College	Wilmore, KY	Eagles
Ashland University	Ashland, OH	Eagles
Assumption College	Worcester, MA	Greyhounds
Athens State University	Athens, AL	Bears
Atlanta Christian College	East Point, GA	Chargers
Atlantic, College of the	Bar Harbor, ME	Black Flies
Atlantic Union College	S. Lancaster, MA	Flames
Auburn University	Auburn, AL	Tigers
Auburn University–Montgomery	Montgomery, AL	Senators
Augsburg College	Minneapolis, MN	Auggies
Augusta State University	Augusta, GA	Jaguars
Augustana College	Rock Island, IL	Vikings/Vi Queens
Augustana College	Sioux Falls, SD	Vikings
Aurora University	Aurora, IL	Spartans
Austin College	Sherman, TX	Kangaroos
Austin Peay State University	Clarksville, TN	Governors
Averett College	Danville, VA	Cougars
Avila College	Kansas City, MO	Eagles
Azusa Pacific College	Azusa, CA	Cougars

B

Babson College	Babson Park, MA	Beavers
Bacone College	Muskogee, OK	Warriors
Baker University	Baldwin, KS	Wildcats
Baldwin-Wallace College	Berea, OH	Yellow Jackets
Ball State University	Muncie, IN	Cardinals
Baptist Bible College	Clarks Summit, PA	Defenders

Senior Colleges and Universities—United States
Alphabetic Listing by Institution

Institution Name	Location	Nickname/Mascot
Baptist Bible College	Springfield, MO	Patriots
Baptist Christian College	Shreveport, LA	Warriors
Barat College	Lake Forest, IL	Bulldogs
Barber-Scotia College	Concord, NC	Sabers
Barclay College	Haviland, KS	Bears
Bard College	Annandale-on-Hudson, NY	Blazers
Barnard College (Women)	New York, NY	Lions
Barry University	Miami, FL	Buccaneers
Bartlesville Wesleyan College	Bartlesville, OK	Eagles
Barton College	Wilson, NC	Bulldogs
Bates College	Lewiston, ME	Bobcats
Bay Path College (Women)	Longmeadow, MA	Wildcats
Bay Ridge Christian College	Kendleton, TX	Eagles
Baylor University	Waco, TX	Bears
Becker College	Worcester, MA	Hawks
Belhaven College	Jackson, MS	Blazers
Bellarmine College	Louisville, KY	Knights
Bellevue University	Bellevue, NE	Bruins
Belmont University	Nashville, TN	Bruins
Belmont Abbey College	Belmont, NC	Crusaders
Beloit College	Beloit, WI	Buccaneers
Bemidji State University	Bemidji, MN	Beavers
Benedict College	Columbia, SC	Tigers
Benedictine College	Atchison, KS	Ravens
Benedictine University	Lisle, IL	Eagles
Bennett College (Women)	Greensboro, NC	Belles
Bentley College	Waltham, MA	Falcons
Berea College	Berea, KY	Mountaineers
Berkeley College	New York, NY	Blaze
Bernard M. Baruch College of CUNY	New York, NY	Statesmen
Berry College	Mt. Berry, GA	Vikings
Bethany College	Bethany, WV	Bison
Bethany College	Lindsborg, KS	Swedes
Bethany College	Scotts Valley, CA	Bruins
Bethany Lutheran College	Mankato, MN	Vikings
Bethel College	McKenzie, TN	Wildcats
Bethel College	Mishawaka, IN	Pilots
Bethel College	N. Newton, KS	Threshers
Bethel College and Seminary	St. Paul, MN	Royals
Bethune-Cookman College	Daytona Beach, FL	Wildcats
Biola University	Mirada, CA	Eagles
Birmingham-Southern College	Birmingham, AL	Panthers

Senior Colleges and Universities—United States
Alphabetic Listing by Institution

Institution Name	Location	Nickname/Mascot
Black Hills State University	Spearfish, ND	Yellow Jackets
Blackburn College	Carlinville, IL	Battlin' Beavers
Bloomfield College	Bloomfield, NJ	Deacons
Bloomsburg University of PA	Bloomsburg, PA	Huskies
Blue Mountain College (Women)	Blue Mountain, MS	Toppers
Bluefield College	Bluefield, VA	Ramblin' Rams
Bluefield State College	Bluefield, WV	Big Blues
Bluffton College	Bluffton, OH	Beavers
Boise State University	Boise, ID	Broncos
Boston Baptist College	Boston, MA	Revolution
Boston College	Chestnut Hill, MA	Eagles
Boston University	Boston, MA	Terriers
Bowdoin College	Brunswick, ME	Polar Bears
Bowie State University	Bowie, MD	Bulldogs
Bowling Green State University	Bowling Green, OH	Falcons
Bradley University	Peoria, IL	Braves
Brandeis University	Waltham, MA	Judges
Brenau University (Women)	Gainesville, GA	Golden Tigers
Brescia College	Owensboro, KY	Bearcats
Brevard College	Brevard, NC	Tornados
Brewton-Parker College	Mt. Vernon, GA	Wildcats
Briar Cliff University	Sioux City, IA	Chargers
Bridgeport, University of	Bridgeport, CT	Purple Knights
Bridgewater College	Bridgewater, VA	Eagles
Bridgewater State College	Bridgewater, MA	Bears
Brigham Young University	Provo, UT	Cougars
Brigham Young University–Hawaii	Laie, HI	Seasiders
Brooklyn College of CUNY	Brooklyn, NY	Bridges, The
Brown University	Providence, RI	Bears
Bryan College	Dayton, TN	Lions
Bryant College	Smithfield, RI	Bulldogs
Bryn Mawr College (Women)	Bryn Mawr, PA	Mawrters
Bucknell University	Lewisburg, PA	Bison
Buena Vista University	Storm Lake, IA	Beavers
Butler University	Indianapolis, IN	Bulldogs

C

Institution Name	Location	Nickname/Mascot
Cabrini College	Radnor, PA	Cavaliers
Cal–Berkeley, University of	Berkeley, CA	Golden Bears
Cal–Davis, University of	Davis, CA	Aggies
Cal–Irvine, University of	Irvine, CA	Anteaters

Senior Colleges and Universities—United States
Alphabetic Listing by Institution

Institution Name	Location	Nickname/Mascot
Cal–Los Angeles, University of (UCLA)	Los Angeles, CA	Bruins
Cal–Riverside, University of	Riverside, CA	Highlanders
Cal–San Diego, University of	La Jolla, CA	Tritons
Cal–Santa Barbara, University of	Santa Barbara, CA	Gauchos
Cal–Santa Cruz, University of	Santa Cruz, CA	Banana Slugs
Cal State University–Bakersfield	Bakersfield, CA	Roadrunners
Cal State University–Chico	Chico, CA	Wildcats
Cal State University–Dominguez Hills	Dominguez Hills, CA	Toros
Cal State University–Fresno State	Fresno, CA	Bulldogs
Cal State University–Fullerton	Fullerton, CA	Titans
Cal State University–Hayward	Hayward, CA	Pioneers
Cal State University–Long Beach State	Long Beach, CA	49ers
Cal State University–Los Angeles	Los Angeles, CA	Golden Eagles
Cal State University–Monterey Bay	Seaside, CA	Otters
Cal State University–Northridge	Northridge, CA	Matadors
Cal State University–Sacramento State	Sacramento, CA	Hornets
Cal State University–San Bernadino	San Bernadino, CA	Coyotes
Cal State University–San Diego State	San Diego, CA	Aztecs
Cal State University–San Jose State	San Jose, CA	Spartans
Cal State University–San Marcos	San Marcos, CA	Cougars
Cal State University–Stanislaus	Turlock, CA	Warriors
Cal State Poly University–Pomona	Pomona, CA	Broncos
Caldwell College	Caldwell, NJ	Cougars
California Baptist University	Riverside, CA	Lancers
California Christian College	Fresno, CA	Runnin' Royals
California Institute of Technology	Pasadena, CA	Beavers
California Lutheran University	Thousand Oaks, CA	Kingsmen/Regals
California Maritime Academy	Vallejo, CA	Keelhaulers
California Poly University–SLO	San Luis Obispo, CA	Mustangs
California University of PA	California, PA	Vulcans
Calumet College of St. Joseph	Whiting, IN	Crimson Wave
Calvary Bible College	Kansas City, MO	Warriors
Calvin College	Grand Rapids, MI	Knights
Cameron University	Lawton, OK	Aggies
Campbell University	Buies Creek, NC	Camels
Campbellsville University	Campbellsville, KY	Tigers
Canisius College	Buffalo, NY	Golden Griffins
Capital University	Columbus, OH	Crusaders
Capitol College	Laurel, MD	Chargers
Cardinal Stritch University	Milwaukee, WI	Crusaders
Carleton College	Northfield, MN	Knights
Carlow College (Women)	Pittsburgh, PA	Celtics

Senior Colleges and Universities—United States
Alphabetic Listing by Institution

Institution Name	Location	Nickname/Mascot
Carnegie-Mellon University	Pittsburgh, PA	Tartans or Skibos
Carroll College	Helena, MT	Fighting Saints
Carroll College	Waukesha, WI	Pioneers
Carson-Newman College	Jefferson City, TN	Eagles
Carthage College	Kenosha, WI	Redmen
Carver Bible College	Atlanta, GA	Cougars
Cascade College	Portland, OR	Thunderbirds
Case Western Reserve University	Cleveland, OH	Spartans
Castleton State College	Castleton, VT	Spartans
Catawba College	Salisbury, NC	Indians
Catholic University of America	Washington, DC	Cardinals
Cazenovia College	Cazenovia, NY	Wildcats
Cedar Crest College (Women)	Allentown, PA	Falcons
Cedarville University	Cedarville, OH	Yellow Jackets
Centenary College of Louisiana	Shreveport, LA	Gents/Ladies
Centenary College	Hackettstown, NJ	Cyclones
Central Arkansas, University of	Conway, AR	Bears
Central Baptist College	Conway, AR	Mustangs
Central Bible College	Springfield, MO	Spartans
Central Christian College of Kansas	McPherson, KS	Tigers
Central Christian College of the Bible	Moberly, MO	Heralds
Central College	Pella, IA	Dutch
Central Connecticut State University	New Britain, CT	Blue Devils
Central Florida, University of	Orlando, FL	Golden Knights
Central Methodist College	Fayette, MO	Eagles
Central Michigan University	Mt. Pleasant, MI	Chippewas
Central Missouri State University	Warrensburg, MO	Mules/Jennies
Central Oklahoma, University of	Edmond, OK	Bronchos
Central State University	Wilberforce, OH	Marauders
Central Washington University	Ellensburg, WA	Wildcats
Centre College	Danville, KY	Colonels
Chadron State College	Chadron, NE	Eagles
Chaminade University of Honolulu	Honolulu, HI	Silverswords
Champlain College	Burlington, VT	Beavers
Chapman University	Orange, CA	Panthers
Charleston, College of	Charleston, SC	Cougars
Charleston, University of	Charleston, WV	Golden Eagles
Charleston Southern University	Charleston, SC	Buccaneers
Chatham College (Women)	Pittsburgh, PA	Cougars
Cheney University	Cheney, PA	Wolves
Chestnut Hill College	Philadelphia, PA	Griffins
Chicago, University of	Chicago, IL	Maroons

8

Senior Colleges and Universities—United States
Alphabetic Listing by Institution

Institution Name	Location	Nickname/Mascot
Chicago State University	Chicago, IL	Cougars
Chowan College	Murfreesboro, NC	Braves
Christendom College	Winchester, VA	Crusaders
Christian Brothers University	Memphis, TN	Buccaneers
Christian Heritage College	El Cajon, CA	Hawks
Christopher Newport University	Newport News, VA	Captains
Cincinnati, University of	Cincinnati, OH	Bearcats
Cincinnati–Clermont, University of	Batavia, OH	Cougars
Cincinnati Bible College & Seminary	Cincinnati, OH	Golden Eagles
Circleville Bible College	Circleville, OH	Crusaders
Citadel, The	Charleston, SC	Bulldogs
City College of NY (CCNY) of CUNY	New York, NY	Beavers
Claflin College	Orangeburg, SC	Panthers
Claremont-Mudd-Scripps College	Claremont, CA	Stags/Athenas
Clarion University	Clarion, PA	Golden Eagles
Clark University	Worcester, MA	Cougars
Clark Atlanta University	Atlanta, GA	Panthers
Clarke College	Dubuque, IA	Crusaders
Clarkson University	Potsdam, NY	Golden Knights
Clayton College and State University	Morrow, GA	Lakers
Clearwater Christian College	Clearwater, FL	Cougars
Clemson University	Clemson, SC	Tigers
Cleveland State University	Cleveland, OH	Vikings
Coastal Carolina University	Conway, SC	Chanticleers
Coe College	Cedar Rapids, IA	Kohawks
Coker College	Hartsville, SC	Cobras
Colby College	Waterville, ME	White Mules
Colby-Sawyer College	New London, NH	Chargers
Colgate University	Hamilton, NY	Raiders
Colorado College	Colorado Springs, CO	Tigers
Colorado, University of	Boulder, CO	Buffaloes
Colorado–Colorado Springs, University of	Colorado Springs, CO	Mountain Lions
Colorado Christian University	Lakewood, CO	Cougars
Colorado School of Mines	Golden, CO	Orediggers
Colorado State University	Ft. Collins, CO	Rams
Columbia College	Columbia, MO	Cougars
Columbia College (Women)	Columbia, SC	Fighting Koalas
Columbia University/Barnard	New York, NY	Lions
Columbia Union College	Takoma Park, MD	Pioneers
Columbus State University	Columbus, GA	Cougars
Concord College	Athens, WV	Mountain Lions
Concordia College	Bronxville, NY	Clippers

Senior Colleges and Universities—United States
Alphabetic Listing by Institution

Institution Name	Location	Nickname/Mascot
Concordia College	Moorhead, MI	Cobbers
Concordia College	Selma, AL	Hornets
Concordia Seminary	St. Louis, MO	Preachers
Concordia Theological Seminary	Ft. Wayne, IN	King's Men
Concordia University	Ann Arbor, MI	Cardinals
Concordia University	Portland, OR	Cavaliers
Concordia University	River Forest, IL	Cougars
Concordia University	St. Paul, MN	Golden Bears
Concordia University at Austin	Austin, TX	Tornados
Concordia University of California	Irvine, CA	Eagles
Concordia University of Nebraska	Seward, NE	Bulldogs
Concordia University, Wisconsin	Mequon, WI	Falcons
Connecticut College	New London, CT	Camels
Connecticut, University of	Storrs, CT	Huskies
Converse College (Women)	Spartanburg, SC	All-Stars
Cooper Union	New York, NY	Pioneers
Coppin State College	Baltimore, MD	Eagles
Cornell College	Mount Vernon, IA	Rams
Cornell University	Ithaca, NY	Big Red
Cornerstone University	Grand Rapids, MI	Golden Eagles
Covenant College	Lookout Mountain, GA	Scots
Creighton University	Omaha, NE	Bluejays
Crichton College	Memphis, TN	Cardinals
Crown College	Powell, TN	Royal Crusaders
Crown College	St. Bonifacius, MN	Purple Storm
Culver-Stockton College	Canton, MO	Wildcats
Cumberland College	Williamsburg, KY	Patriots
Cumberland University	Lebanon, TN	Bulldogs
Curry College	Milton, MA	Colonels
Cypress College	Cypress, CA	Chargers

D

Institution Name	Location	Nickname/Mascot
D'Youville College	Buffalo, NY	Spartans
Daemen College	Amherst, NY	Warriors
Dakota State University	Madison, SD	Trojans
Dakota Wesleyan University	Mitchell, SD	Tigers
Dallas, University of	Irving, TX	Crusaders
Dallas Baptist University	Dallas, TX	Patriots
Dallas Bible College	Dallas, TX	Eagles
Dallas Christian College	Dallas, TX	Crusaders
Dana College	Blair, NE	Vikings

Senior Colleges and Universities—United States
Alphabetic Listing by Institution

Institution Name	Location	Nickname/Mascot
Daniel Webster College	Nashua, NH	Eagles
Dartmouth College	Hanover, NH	Big Green
Davidson College	Davidson, NC	Wildcats
Davis & Elkins College	Elkins, WV	Senators
Dayton, University of	Dayton, OH	Flyers
Defiance College	Defiance, OH	Yellow Jackets
Delaware, University of	Newark, DE	Fightin' Blue Hens
Delaware State University	Dover, DE	Hornets
Delaware Valley College	Doylestown, PA	Aggies
Delta State University	Cleveland, MS	Statesmen
Denison University	Granville, OH	Big Red
Denver, University of + Women's College of the University of Denver	Denver, CO	Pioneers
DePaul University	Chicago, IL	Blue Demons
DePauw University	Greencastle, IN	Tigers
DeSales University	Center Valley, PA	Bulldogs
Detroit Bible College	Farmington Hills, MI	Lancers
Detroit College of Business	Dearborn, MI	Falcons
Detroit Mercy, University of	Detroit, MI	Titans
DeVry Institute of Technology	Atlanta, GA	Hoyas
Dickinson College	Carlisle, PA	Red Devils
Dickinson State University	Dickinson, ND	Blue Hawks
Dillard University	New Orleans, LA	Blue Devils
District of Columbia, University of the	Washington, DC	Firebirds
Doane College	Doane, NE	Tigers
Dominican College	Orangeburg, NY	Chargers
Dominican University	River Forest, IL	Stars
Dominican University of California	San Rafael, CA	Penguins
Dordt College	Sioux Center, IA	Defenders
Dowling College	Oakdale, NY	Golden Lions
Drake University	Des Moines, IA	Bulldogs
Drew University	Madison, NJ	Rangers
Drexel University	Philadelphia, PA	Dragons
Drury College	Springfield, MO	Panthers
Dubuque, University of	Dubuque, IA	Spartans
Duke University	Durham, NC	Blue Devils
Duquesne University	Pittsburgh, PA	Dukes

E

Earlham College	Richmond, IN	Quakers
East Carolina University	Greenville, NC	Pirates
East Central University	Ada, OK	Tigers

Senior Colleges and Universities—United States
Alphabetic Listing by Institution

Institution Name	Location	Nickname/Mascot
East Coast Bible College	Charlotte, NC	Cavaliers
East Stroudsburg University	East Stroudsburg, PA	Warriors
East Tennessee State University	Johnson City, TN	Buccaneers
East Texas Baptist University	Marshall, TX	Tigers
East Texas State University	Commerce, TX	Lions
East-West University	Chicago, IL	Phantoms
Eastern University	St. Davids, PA	Eagles
Eastern Connecticut State University	Willimantic, CT	Warriors
Eastern Illinois University	Charleston, IL	Panthers
Eastern Kentucky University	Richmond, KY	Colonels
Eastern Mennonite University	Harrisonburg, VA	Royals
Eastern Michigan University	Ypsilanti, MI	Eagles
Eastern Montana College	Billings, MT	Yellowjackets
Eastern Nazarene College	Quincy, MA	Crusaders
Eastern New Mexico University	Portales, NM	Greyhounds
Eastern Oregon University	La Grande, OR	Mountaineers
Eastern Washington University	Cheney, WA	Eagles
Eckerd College	St. Petersburg, FL	Tritons
Edgewood College	Madison, WI	Eagles
Edinboro University of Pennsylvania	Edinboro, PA	Fighting Scots
Edward Waters College	Jacksonville, FL	Fighting Tigers
Eisenhower College	Seneca Falls, NY	Generals
Elizabeth City State University	Elizabeth City, NC	Vikings
Elizabethtown College	Elizabethtown, PA	Blue Jays
Elmhurst College	Elmhurst, IL	Blue Jays
Elmira College	Elmira, NY	Soaring Eagles
Elms College	Chicopee, MA	Blazers
Elon University	Elon College, NC	Phoenix
Embry-Riddle Aeronautical University	Daytona Beach, FL	Eagles
Embry-Riddle Aeronautical University	Prescott, AZ	Eagles
Emerson—Mass. College of Art	Boston, MA	Lions
Emmanuel College	Boston, MA	Saints
Emmanuel College	Franklin Springs, GA	Lions
Emmaus Bible College	Dubuque, IA	Eagles
Emory University	Atlanta, GA	Eagles
Emory & Henry College	Emory, VA	Wasps
Emporia State University	Emporia, KS	Hornets
Endicott College	Beverly, MA	Power Gulls
Erskine College	Due West, SC	Flying Fleet/Lady Fleet
Eugene Bible College	Eugene, OR	Deacons
Eureka College	Eureka, IL	Red Devils
Evangel University	Springfield, MO	Crusaders

Senior Colleges and Universities—United States
Alphabetic Listing by Institution

Institution Name	Location	Nickname/Mascot
Evansville, University of	Evansville, IN	Purple Aces
Evergreen State College	Olympia, WA	Geoducks

F

Institution Name	Location	Nickname/Mascot
Fairleigh-Dickinson University—Florham	Madison, NJ	Devils
Fairleigh-Dickinson University—Teaneck	Teaneck, NJ	Knights
Fairfield University	Fairfield, CT	Stags
Fairhaven Baptist College	Chesterton, IN	Fundamentalists
Fairmont State College	Fairmont, WV	Falcons
Faith Baptist Bible College	Ankeny, IA	Eagles
Faulkner University	Montgomery, AL	Eagles
Fayetteville State University	Fayetteville, NC	Broncos
Felician College	Lodi, NJ	Golden Falcons
Ferris State University	Big Rapids, MI	Bulldogs
Ferrum College	Ferrum, VA	Panthers
Findlay, University of	Findlay, OH	Oilers
Finlandia University	Hancock, MI	Lions
Fisher College	Boston, MA	Falcons
Fisk University	Nashville, TN	Bulldogs
Fitchburg State College	Fitchburg, MA	Falcons
Five Towns College	Dix Hills, NY	The Sound or "Sharky"
Flagler College	St. Augustine, FL	Saints
Florida, University of	Gainesville, FL	Gators
Florida A & M University	Tallahassee, FL	Rattlers
Florida Atlantic University	Boca Raton, FL	Owls
Florida Christian College	Kissimmee, FL	Suns
Florida Gulf Coast University	Ft. Myers, FL	Eagles
Florida Institute of Technology	Melbourne, FL	Panthers
Florida International University	Miami, FL	Golden Panthers
Florida Memorial College	Opa Locka, FL	Lions
Florida Southern College	Lakeland, FL	Moccasins
Florida State University	Tallahassee, FL	Seminoles
Fontbonne College	St. Louis, MO	Griffins
Fordham University	New York, NY	Rams
Fort Hays State University	Fort Hays, KS	Tigers
Fort Lauderdale College	Fort Lauderdale, FL	Seagulls
Fort Lewis College	Durango, CO	Skyhawks
Fort Valley State University	Fort Valley, GA	Wildcats
Framingham State College	Framingham, MA	Rams
Francis Marion University	Florence, SC	Patriots
Franklin College	Franklin, IN	Grizzlies
Franklin & Marshall College	Lancaster, PA	Diplomats

Senior Colleges and Universities—United States
Alphabetic Listing by Institution

Institution Name	Location	Nickname/Mascot
Franklin Pierce College	Rindge, NH	Ravens
Free Will Baptist Bible College	Nashville, TN	Flames
Freed-Hardeman University	Henderson, TN	Lions
Fresno Pacific College	Fresno, CA	Sunbirds
Friends University	Wichita, KS	Falcons
Frostburg State University	Frostburg, MD	Bobcats
Furman University	Greenville, SC	Palladins

G

Institution Name	Location	Nickname/Mascot
Gallaudet University	Washington, DC	Bison
Gannon University	Erie, PA	Golden Knights
Gardner-Webb University	Boiling Springs, NC	Bulldogs
Geneva College	Beaver Falls, PA	Golden Tornadoes
George Fox University	Newberg, OR	Bruins
George Mason University	Fairfax, VA	Patriots
George Washington University	Washington, DC	Colonials
Georgetown College	Georgetown, KY	Tigers
Georgetown University	Washington, DC	Hoyas
Georgia, University of	Athens, GA	Bulldogs
Georgia College and State University	Milledgeville, GA	Colonials
Georgia Institute of Tech. (Ga. Tech)	Atlanta, GA	Yellow Jackets
Georgia Southern University	Statesboro, GA	Eagles
Georgia Southwestern State University	Americus, GA	Hurricanes
Georgia State University	Atlanta, GA	Panthers
Georgian Court College (Women)	Lakewood, NJ	Lions
Gettysburg College	Gettysburg, PA	Bullets
Glenville State College	Glenville, WV	Pioneers
Golden Gate University	San Francisco, CA	Golden Griffins
Golden State Baptist College	Santa Clara, CA	Bears
Goldey-Beacom College	Wilmington, DE	Lightning
Gonzaga University	Spokane, WA	Bulldogs
Gordon College	Wenham, MA	Fighting Scots
Goshen College	Goshen, IN	Maple Leafs
Goucher College	Baltimore, MD	Gophers
Grace Bible College	Wyoming, MI	Tigers
Grace College & Seminary	Winona Lake, IN	Lancers
Grace University	Omaha, NE	Royals
Graceland University	Lamoni, IA	Yellowjackets
Grambling State University	Grambling, LA	Tigers
Grand Canyon University	Phoenix, AZ	Antelopes
Grand Rapids Bible/Music College	Grand Rapids, MI	Victors
Grand Valley State University	Allendale, MI	Lakers

Senior Colleges and Universities—United States
Alphabetic Listing by Institution

Institution Name	Location	Nickname/Mascot
Grand View College	Des Moines, IA	Vikings
Great Falls, University of	Great Falls, MT	Argonauts
Great Lakes Christian College	Lansing, MI	Crusaders
Green Mountain College	Poultney, VT	Eagles
Greensboro College	Greensboro, NC	Pride, The
Greenville College	Greenville, IL	Panthers
Grinnell College	Grinnell, IA	Pioneers
Grove City College	Grove City, PA	Wolverines
Guilford College	Greensboro, NC	Quakers
Gustavus Adolphus College	St. Peter, MN	Golden Gusties
Gwynedd Mercy College	Gwynedd Valley, PA	Griffins

H

Institution Name	Location	Nickname/Mascot
Hamilton College	Clinton, NY	Continentals
Hamline University	St. Paul, MN	Pipers
Hampden-Sydney College	Farmville, VA	Tigers
Hampton University	Hampton, VA	Pirates
Hannibal-LaGrange College	Hannibal, MO	Trojans
Hanover College	Hanover, IN	Panthers
Hardin-Baylor University	Belton, TX	Crusaders
Hardin-Simmons University	Abilene, TX	Cowboys/Cowgirls
Harding University	Searcy, AR	Bison
Harris-Stowe State College	St. Louis, MO	Hornets
Hartford, University of + Hartford College for Women	West Hartford, CT	Hawks
Hartwick College	Oneonta, NY	Hawks
Harvard University	Cambridge, MA	Crimson
Haskell Indian Nations University	Lawrence, KS	Fightin' Indians
Hastings College	Hastings, NE	Broncos
Haverford College	Haverford, PA	Fords
Hawaii (Manoa), University of (All sports except men's basketball)	Honolulu, HI	Rainbows/Rainbow Wahine
Hawaii (Manoa), University of (Men's basketball)	Honolulu, HI	Rainbow Warriors
Hawaii—Hilo, University of	Hilo, HI	Vulcans
Hawaii Pacific University	Honolulu, HI	Sea Warriors
Heidelberg College	Tiffin, OH	Berg, The
Hellenic College	Brookline, MA	Owls
Henderson State University	Arkadelphia, AR	Reddies
Hendrix College	Conway, AR	Warriors
Heritage College	Orlando, FL	Minutemen

Senior Colleges and Universities—United States
Alphabetic Listing by Institution

Institution Name	Location	Nickname/Mascot
High Point University	High Point, NC	Panthers
Hilbert College	Hamburg, NY	Hawks
Hillsdale College	Hillsdale, MI	Chargers
Hillsdale Free Will Baptist College	Moore, OK	Saints
Hiram College	Hiram, OH	Terriers
Hobart College	Geneva, NY	Statesmen
Hofstra University	Hempstead, NY	Pride
Hollins University (Women)	Roanoke, VA	Green & Gold
Holy Cross, College of the	Worcester, MA	Crusaders
Holy Family College	Philadelphia, PA	Tigers
Holy Names College	Oakland, CA	Hawks
Hood College	Frederick, MD	Blazers
Hope College	Hope, MI	Flying Dutch
Hope International University	Fullerton, CA	Royals
Houghton College	Houghton, NY	Highlanders
Houston, University of	Houston, TX	Cougars
Houston Baptist University	Houston, TX	Huskies
Howard University	Washington, DC	Bison
Howard Payne University	Brownwood, TX	Yellow Jackets
Humboldt State University	Arcata, CA	Lumberjacks
Hunter College of CUNY	New York, NY	Hawks
Huntingdon College	Montgomery, AL	Hawks
Huntington College	Huntington, IN	Foresters
(Si Tanka) Huron University	Huron, SD	Screaming Eagles
Husson College	Bangor, ME	Braves
Huston-Tillotson College	Austin, TX	Rams

I

Institution Name	Location	Nickname/Mascot
Idaho, University of	Moscow, ID	Vandals
Idaho State University	Pocatello, ID	Bengals
Illinois, University of	Urbana/Champagne, IL	Fighting Illini
Illinois College	Jacksonville, IL	Blueboys/Lady Blues
Illinois—Chicago, University of	Chicago, IL	Flames
Illinois at Springfield, University of	Springfield, IL	Prairie Stars
Illinois State University	Normal, IL	Redbirds
Illinois Institute of Technology	Chicago, IL	Scarlet Hawks
Illinois Wesleyan University	Bloomington, IL	Titans
Immaculata College (Women)	Immaculata, PA	Mighty Macs
Immanuel Lutheran College	Eau Claire, WI	Knights
Incarnate Word, University of the	San Antonio, TX	Crusaders

Senior Colleges and Universities—United States
Alphabetic Listing by Institution

Institution Name	Location	Nickname/Mascot
Indiana Institute of Technology	Fort Wayne, IN	Warriors
Indiana State University—Terre Haute	Terra Haute, IN	Sycamores
Indiana University	Bloomington, IN	Hoosiers
Indiana University—Kokomo	Kokomo, IN	Knights
Indiana University—Northwest	Gary, IN	RedHawks
Indiana University—South Bend	South Bend, IN	Titans
Indiana University—Purdue University Indianapolis	Indianapolis, IN	Jaguars
Indiana University—Purdue University	Fort Wayne, IN	Mastodons
Indiana University—Southeast	New Albany, IN	Grenadiers
Indiana University of Pennsylvania	Indiana, PA	Indians
Indiana Wesleyan University	Marion, IN	Wildcats
Indianapolis, University of	Indianapolis, IN	Greyhounds
Iona College	New Rochelle, NY	Gaels
Iowa, University of	Iowa City, IA	Hawkeyes
Iowa State University	Ames, IA	Cyclones
Iowa Wesleyan College	Mt. Pleasant, IA	Tigers
Ithaca College	Ithaca, NY	Bombers

J

Institution Name	Location	Nickname/Mascot
Jackson State University	Jackson, MS	Tigers
Jacksonville University	Jacksonville, FL	Dolphins
Jacksonville State University	Jacksonville, AL	Gamecocks
James Madison University	Harrisonburg, VA	Dukes
Jamestown College	Jamestown, ND	Jimmies
Jarvis Christian College	Hawkins, TX	Bulldogs
Jimmy Swaggart Bible College	Baton Rouge, LA	Eagles
John Brown University	Siloam Springs, AR	Golden Eagles
John Carroll University	Cleveland, OH	Blue Streaks
John Jay College of Criminal Justice of CUNY	New York, NY	Bloodhounds
John Wesley College	High Point, NC	Crusaders
Johns Hopkins University	Baltimore, MD	Blue Jays
Johnson & Wales University	Charleston, SC	Wildcats
Johnson & Wales University	N. Miami, FL	Wildcats
Johnson & Wales University	Providence, RI	Wildcats
Johnson Bible College	Knoxville, TN	Preachers/Evangels
Johnson C. Smith University	Charlotte, NC	Golden Bulls
Johnson State College	Johnson, VT	Badgers
Josephinum College	Columbus, OH	Vikings
Judson College	Elgin, IL	Eagles

Senior Colleges and Universities—United States
Alphabetic Listing by Institution

Institution Name	Location	Nickname/Mascot
Judson College for Women	Marion, AL	Lady Eagles
Juniata College	Huntingdon, PA	Eagles

K

Institution Name	Location	Nickname/Mascot
Kalamazoo College	Kalamazoo, MI	Hornets
Kansas, University of	Lawrence, KS	Jayhawks
Kansas City College & Bible School	Overland Park, KS	Falcons
Kansas State University	Manhattan, KS	Wildcats
Kansas Wesleyan University	Salina, KS	Coyotes
Kean University	Union, NJ	Cougars
Keene State College	Keene, NH	Owls
Kendall College	Evanston, IL	Vikings
Kennesaw State University	Marietta, GA	Owls
Kent State University	Kent, OH	Golden Flashes
Kent State University–Ashtabula	Ashtabula, OH	Vikings
Kent State University–Salem	Salem, OH	Cougars
Kent State University–Stark	Canton, OH	Cobras
Kent State University–Trumbull	Warren, OH	Titans
Kent State University–Tuscawaras	New Philadelphia, OH	Kubs
Kentucky, University of	Lexington, KY	Wildcats
Kentucky Christian College	Grayson, KY	Knights
Kentucky State University	Frankfort, KY	Thorobreds/Thorobrettes
Kentucky Wesleyan College	Owensboro, KY	Panthers
Kenyon College	Gambier, OH	Lords/Ladies
Keuka College	Keuka Park, NY	Warriors
Keystone College	La Plume, PA	Giants
King College	Bristol, TN	Tornados
King's College	Wilkes-Barre, PA	Monarchs
Knox College	Galesburg, IL	Prairie Fire
Knoxville College	Knoxville, TN	Bulldogs
Kutztown University	Kutztown, PA	Golden Bears

L

Institution Name	Location	Nickname/Mascot
La Roche College	Pittsburgh, PA	Red Hawks
La Salle University	Philadelphia, PA	Explorers
La Sierra University	Riverside, CA	Golden Eagles
La Verne, University of	La Verne, CA	Leopards
Lafayette College	Easton, PA	Leopards
LaGrange College	La Grange, GA	Panthers

Senior Colleges and Universities—United States
Alphabetic Listing by Institution

Institution Name	Location	Nickname/Mascot
Lake Erie College	Painesville, OH	Storm
Lake Forest College	Lake Forest, IL	Foresters
Lake Superior State University	Sault Ste. Marie, MI	Lakers
Lakeland College	Sheboygan, WI	Muskies
Lakewood College	Lakewood, OH	Lakers
Lamar University	Beaumont, TX	Cardinals
Lambuth University	Jackson, TN	Eagles
Lancaster Bible College	Lancaster, PA	Chargers
Lander University	Greenwood, SC	Senators
Lane College	Jackson, TN	Dragons
Langston University	Langston, OK	Lions
Lasell College	Newton, MA	Lasers
Latin American Bible Institute	LaPuente, CA	Lions
Lawrence Technical University	Southfield, MI	Blue Devils
Lawrence University	Appleton, WI	Vikings
Le Moyne College	Syracuse, NY	Dolphins
LeMoyne-Owen College	Memphis, TN	Magicians
Lebanon Valley College	Annville, PA	Flying Dutchmen
Lee University	Cleveland, TN	Flames
Lees-McRae College	Banner Elk, NC	Bobcats
Lehigh University	Bethlehem, PA	Mountain Hawks
Lehman College of CUNY	Bronx, NY	Lightning
Lenoir-Rhyne College	Hickory, NC	Bears
Lesley University	Cambridge, MA	Lynx
LeTourneau University	Longview, TX	Yellowjackets
Lewis University	Romeoville, IL	Flyers
Lewis & Clark College	Portland, OR	Pioneers
Lewis-Clark State College	Lewiston, ID	Warriors
Liberty University	Lynchburg, VA	Flames
LIFE Pacific College	San Dimas, CA	Warriors
LIFE University	Marietta, GA	Running Eagles
Limestone College	Gaffney, SC	Saints
Lincoln University	Jefferson City, MO	Blue Tigers
Lincoln University	Philadelphia, PA	Lions
Lincoln Christian College & Seminary	Lincoln, IL	Preachers
Lincoln Memorial University	Harrogate, TN	Railsplitters
Lindenwood University	St. Charles, MO	Lions
Lindsey Wilson College	Columbia, KY	Blue Raiders
Linfield College	McMinnville, OR	Wildcats
Lipscomb University	Nashville, TN	Bison
Livingstone College	Salisbury, NC	Blue Bears
Lock Haven University of Pennsylvania	Lock Haven, PA	Bald Eagles

Senior Colleges and Universities—United States
Alphabetic Listing by Institution

Institution Name	Location	Nickname/Mascot
Long Island University	Greenvale, NY	Blackbirds
Long Island University—Brooklyn Campus	Brooklyn, NY	Blackbirds
Long Island University—CW Post Campus	Brookville, NY	Pioneers
Long Island University—Southhampton	Southhampton, NY	Colonials
Longwood College	Farmville, VA	Lancers
Loras College	Dubuque, IA	DuHawks
Louisiana College	Pineville, LA	Wildcats
Louisiana—Monroe, University of	Monroe, LA	Indians
Louisiana at Lafayette, University of	Lafayette, LA	Rajin' Cajuns
Louisiana State University	Baton Rouge, LA	Tigers
Louisiana State University—Shreveport	Shreveport, LA	Pilots
Louisiana Technical University	Ruston, LA	Bulldogs/Lady Techsters
Louisville, University of	Louisville, KY	Cardinals
Loyola of Chicago University	Chicago, IL	Ramblers
Loyola University	New Orleans, LA	Wolfpack
Loyola College	Baltimore, MD	Greyhounds
Loyola Marymount University	Los Angeles, CA	Lions
Lubbock Christian University	Lubbock, TX	Chaparrals
Luther College	Decorah, IA	Norse
Lycoming College	Williamsport, PA	Warriors
Lynchburg College	Lynchburg, VA	Hornets
Lyndon State College	Lyndonville, VT	Hornets
Lynn University	Boca Raton, FL	Knights
Lyon College	Batesville, AR	Scots/Pipers

M

Institution Name	Location	Nickname/Mascot
MacMurray College	Jacksonville, IL	Highlanders
Macalester College	St. Paul, MN	Scots
Madonna University	Livonia, MI	Crusaders
Maine, University of	Orono, ME	Black Bears
Maine—Augusta, University of	Augusta, ME	Rebels
Maine—Farmington, University of	Farmington, ME	Beavers
Maine—Fort Kent, University of	Fort Kent, ME	Bengals
Maine—Machias, University of	Machias, ME	Clippers
Maine—Presque Isle, University of	Presque Isle, ME	Owls
Maine Maritime Academy	Castine, ME	Mariners
Malone College	Canton, OH	Pioneers
Manchester College	N. Manchester, IN	Spartans
Maharishi University of Management	Fairfield, IA	Flyers
Manhattan Christian College	Manhattan, KS	Crusaders
Manhattan College	Bronx, NY	Jaspers

Senior Colleges and Universities—United States
Alphabetic Listing by Institution

Institution Name	Location	Nickname/Mascot
Manhattanville College	Purchase, NY	Valiants
Manna Bible Institute	Philadelphia, PA	Saints
Mansfield University	Mansfield, PA	Mountaineers
Maranatha Baptist Bible College	Watertown, WI	Crusaders
Marian College	Fond du Lac, WI	Sabres
Marian College	Indianapolis, IN	Knights
Marietta College	Marietta, OH	Pioneers
Marist College	Poughkeepsie, NY	Red Foxes
Marquette University	Milwaukee, WI	Golden Eagles
Mars Hill College	Mars Hill, NC	Lions
Marshall University	Huntington, WV	Thundering Herd
Martin Luther College	New Ulm, MN	Knights
Martin Methodist College	Pulaski, TN	RedHawks
Mary, University of	Bismarck, ND	Marauders
Mary Baldwin College (Women)	Staunton, VA	Squirrels
Mary Hardin-Baylor, University of	Belton, TX	Crusaders
Mary Washington College	Fredericksburg, VA	Eagles
Marycrest International University	Davenport, IA	Marauding Eagles
Marygrove College	Detroit, MI	Mustangs
Maryland, University of	College Park, MD	Terrapins
Maryland Baltimore County, University of	Catonsville, MD	Retrievers
Maryland Bible College & Seminary	Baltimore, MD	Eagles
Maryland—Eastern Shore, University of	Princess Anne, MD	Hawks
Marymount College (Women)	Tarrytown, NY	Saints
Marymount University	Arlington, VA	Saints
Maryville College	Maryville, TN	Fighting Scots
Maryville University of St. Louis	St. Louis, MO	Saints
Marywood University	Scranton, PA	Pacers
Massachusetts, University of	Amherst, MA	Minutemen
Massachusetts—Boston, University of	Boston, MA	Beacons
Massachusetts—Dartmouth, University of	N. Dartmouth, MA	Corsairs
Massachusetts—Lowell, University of	Lowell, MA	River Hawks
Mass. College of the Liberal Arts	North Adams, MA	Trailblazers
Mass. College of Pharmacy & Health	Boston, MA	Cardinals
Massachusetts Institute of Technology (MIT)	Cambridge, MA	Engineers
Massachusetts Maritime Academy	Buzzards Bay, MA	Buccaneers
Master's College, The	Santa Clarita, CA	Mustangs
Mayville State University	Mayville, ND	Comet
McCoy College	West Hills, CA	Bald Eagles
McDaniel College	Westminster, MD	Green Terrors
McKendree College	Lebanon, IL	Bearcats
McMurry University	Abilene, TX	Indians

Senior Colleges and Universities—United States
Alphabetic Listing by Institution

Institution Name	Location	Nickname/Mascot
McNeese State University	Lake Charles, LA	Cowboys/Cowgirls
McPherson College	McPherson, KS	Bulldogs
Medaille College	Buffalo, NY	Mavericks
Medgar Evers College of CUNY	Brooklyn, NY	Cougars
Memphis University	Memphis, TN	Tigers
Menlo College	Menlo Park, CA	Oaks
Mercer College	Atlanta, GA	Golden Hawks
Mercer University	Macon, GA	Bears
Mercy College	Dobbs Ferry, NY	Flyers
Mercyhurst College	Erie, PA	Lakers
Meredith College	Raleigh, NC	Angels
Merrimack College	N. Andover, MA	Warriors
Mesa State College	Grand Junction, CO	Mavericks
Messenger College	Joplin, MO	Eagles
Messiah College	Grantham, PA	Falcons
Methodist College	Fayetteville, NC	Monarchs
Metropolitan State College	Denver, CO	Roadrunners
Miami, University of	Miami, FL	Hurricanes
Miami Christian College	Miami, FL	Warriors
Miami University	Oxford, OH	RedHawks
Michigan, University of	Ann Arbor, MI	Wolverines
Michigan--Dearborn, University of	Dearborn, MI	Wolves
Michigan State University	East Lansing, MI	Spartans
Michigan Technical University	Houghton, MI	Huskies
Mid-America Bible College	Oklahoma City, OK	Evangels
Mid-America Nazarene College	Olathe, KS	Pioneers
Mid-Continent College	Mayfield, KY	Cougars
Middle Tennessee State University	Murfreesboro, TN	Blue Raiders
Middlebury College	Middlebury, VT	Panthers
Midland Lutheran College	Fremont, NE	Warriors
Midway College (Women)	Midway, KY	Eagles
Midwest Christian College	Oklahoma City, OK	Conquerors
Midwestern State University	Wichita Falls, TX	Indians
Miles College	Birmingham, AL	Golden Bears
Millersville University	Millersville, PA	Marauders
Milligan College	Milligan College,TN	Buffaloes
Millikin University	Decatur, IL	Big Blue
Mills College (Women)	Oakland, CA	Cyclone
Millsaps College	Jackson, MS	Majors
Milwaukee School of Engineering	Milwaukee, WI	Raiders
Minnesota, University of	Minneapolis, MN	Golden Gophers
Minnesota--Crookston, University of	Crookston, MN	Golden Eagles

Senior Colleges and Universities—United States
Alphabetic Listing by Institution

Institution Name	Location	Nickname/Mascot
Minnesota–Duluth, University of	Duluth, MN	Bulldogs
Minnesota–Morris, University of	Morris, MN	Cougars
Minnesota Bible College	Rochester, MN	Royals
Minnesota State University Mankato	Mankato, MN	Mavericks
Minnesota State University Moorhead	Moorhead, MN	Dragons
Minot State University	Minot, ND	Beavers
Misericordia, College	Dallas, PA	Cougars
Mississippi College	Clinton, MS	Choctaws
Mississippi, University of	Oxford, MS	Rebels
Mississippi State University	Starkville, MS	Bulldogs
Mississippi University for Women	Columbus, MS	Blues
Mississippi Valley State University	Itta Bena, MS	Delta Devils
Missouri, University of	Columbia, MO	Tigers
Missouri–Kansas City, University of	Kansas City, MO	Kangaroos
Missouri–Rolla, University of	Rolla, MO	Miners
Missouri–St. Louis, University of	St. Louis, MO	Rivermen
Missouri Baptist College	St. Louis, MO	Spartans
Missouri Southern State College	Joplin, MO	Lions
Missouri Valley College	Marshall, MO	Vikings
Missouri Western State College	St. Joseph, MO	Griffons
Mitchell College	New London, CT	Pequots
Mobile, University of	Mobile, AL	Rams
Molloy College	Rockville Center, NY	Lions
Monmouth College	Monmouth, IL	Fighting Scots
Monmouth University	W. Long Branch, NJ	Hawks
Montana, University of	Missoula, MT	Grizzlies
Montana State University–Billings	Billings, MT	Yellowjackets
Montana State University–Bozeman	Bozeman, MT	Bobcats
Montana State University–Northern	Havre, MT	Northern Lights/Skylights
Montana Tech of the Univ. of Montana	Butte, MT	Orediggers
Montana Western, University of	Dillon, MT	Bulldogs
Montclair State University	Upper Montclair, NJ	Red Hawks
Montevallo, University of	Montevallo, AL	Falcons
Montreat College	Montreat, NC	Cavaliers
Moody Bible Institute	Chicago, IL	Archers
Moravian College	Bethlehem, PA	Greyhounds
Morehead State University	Morehead, KY	Eagles
Morehouse College	Atlanta, GA	Maroon Tigers
Morgan State University	Baltimore, MD	Golden Bears
Morningside College	Sioux City, IA	Mustangs
Morris College	Sumter, SC	Hornets
Morris Brown College	Atlanta, GA	Wolverines

Senior Colleges and Universities—United States
Alphabetic Listing by Institution

Institution Name	Location	Nickname/Mascot
Mt. Aloysius College	Cresson, PA	Mounties
Mt. Holyoke College (Women)	South Hadley, MA	Lyons
Mt. Ida College	Newton Centre, MA	Mustangs
Mt. Marty College	Yankton, SD	Lancers
Mt. Mary College (Women)	Milwaukee, WI	Crusaders
Mt. Mercy College	Cedar Rapids, IA	Mustangs
Mt. Olive College	Mt. Olive, NC	Trojans
Mt. Senario College	Ladysmith, WI	Fighting Saints
Mt. St. Clare College	Clinton, IA	Mounties
Mt. St. Joseph, College of	Cincinnati, OH	Lions
Mt. St. Mary College	Newburgh, NY	Knights
Mt. St. Mary's College	Emmitsburg, MD	Mountaineers
Mt. St. Mary's College (Women)	Los Angeles, CA	Athenians
Mt. St. Vincent, College of	Riverdale, NY	Dolphins
Mt. Union College	Alliance, OH	Raiders
Mt. Vernon Nazarene College	Mt. Vernon, OH	Cougars
Mountain State University	Beckley, WV	Cougars
Muhlenberg College	Allentown, PA	Mules
Multnomah Bible College	Portland, OR	Ambassadors
Murray State University	Murray, KY	Racers
Muskingum College	New Concord, OH	Fighting Muskies

N

Institution Name	Location	Nickname/Mascot
National American University	Rapid City, SD	Mavericks
National-Louis University	Chicago, IL	Eagles
Nazareth College	Rochester, NY	Golden Flyers
Nebraska, University of	Lincoln, NE	Cornhuskers
Nebraska–Kearney, University of	Kearney, NE	Antelopes
Nebraska–Omaha, University of	Omaha, NE	Mavericks
Nebraska Christian College	Norfolk, NE	Parsons
Nebraska Wesleyan University	Lincoln, NE	Prairie Wolves
Neumann College	Aston, PA	Knights
Nevada, University of	Reno, NV	Wolf Pack
Nevada–Las Vegas, University of (UNLV)	Las Vegas, NV	Runnin' Rebels
New England, University of	Biddeford, ME	Nor'easters
New England College	Henniker, NH	Pilgrims
New Hampshire College	Hooksett, NH	Penmen
New Hampshire, University of	Durham, NH	Wildcats
New Haven, University of	West Haven, CT	Chargers
New Jersey City University	Jersey City, NJ	Gothic Knights
New Jersey, College of	Ewing, NJ	Lions

Senior Colleges and Universities—United States
Alphabetic Listing by Institution

Institution Name	Location	Nickname/Mascot
New Jersey Institute of Technology	Newark, NJ	Highlanders
New Mexico, University of	Albuquerque, NM	Lobos
New Mexico Highlands University	Las Vegas, NM	Cowboys
New Mexico State University	Las Cruces, NM	Aggies
New Orleans, University of	New Orleans, LA	Privateers
New Rochelle (Women), College of	New Rochelle, NY	Blue Angels
New York City Technology College of CUNY	Brooklyn, NY	Yellow Jackets
New York Institute of Technology	Old Westbury, NY	Bears
New York University (NYU)	New York, NY	Violets
Newberry College	Newberry, SC	Indians
Newbury College	Brookline, MA	Nighthawks
Newcomb College	New Orleans, LA	Green Wave
Newman University	Wichita, KS	Jets
Newport News Apprentice Institute	Newport News, VA	Builders
Niagara University	Niagara University, NY	Purple Eagles
Nicholls State University	Thibodaux, LA	Colonels
Nichols College	Dudley, MA	Bison
Norfolk State University	Norfolk, VA	Spartans
North Alabama, University of	Florence, AL	Lions
North Carolina, University of	Chapel Hill, NC	Tar Heels
North Carolina A & T State University	Greensboro, NC	Aggies
North Carolina Central University	Durham, NC	Eagles
North Carolina State University	Raleigh, NC	Wolfpack
North Carolina Wesleyan College	Rocky Mount, NC	Battling Bishops
North Carolina–Asheville, University of	Asheville, NC	Bulldogs
North Carolina–Charlotte, University of	Charlotte, NC	49ers
North Carolina–Greensboro, University of	Greensboro, NC	Spartans
North Carolina–Wilmington, University of	Wilmington, NC	Seahawks
North Central College	Naperville, IL	Cardinals
North Central University	Minneapolis, MN	Rams
North Dakota, University of	Grand Forks, ND	Fighting Sioux
North Dakota State University	Fargo, ND	Bison
North Florida, University of	Jacksonville, FL	Ospreys
North Georgia College & State University	Dahlonega, GA	Saints
North Greenville College	Tigerville, SC	Crusaders
North Park University	Chicago, IL	Vikings
North Texas, University of	Denton, TX	Mean Green
Northeastern Illinois University	Chicago, IL	Golden Eagles
Northeastern State University	Tahlequah, OK	Redmen
Northeastern University	Boston, MA	Huskies
Northern Arizona University	Flagstaff, AZ	Lumberjacks
Northern Colorado, University of	Greeley, CO	Bears

Senior Colleges and Universities—United States
Alphabetic Listing by Institution

Institution Name	Location	Nickname/Mascot
Northern Illinois University	DeKalb, IL	Huskies
Northern Iowa, University of	Cedar Falls, IA	Panthers
Northern Kentucky University	Highland Heights, KY	Norse
Northern Michigan University	Marquette, MI	Wildcats
Northern State University	Aberdeen, SD	Wolves
Northland College	Ashland, WI	Lumberjacks/Lumberjills
Northland Baptist Bible College	Dunbar, WI	Pioneers
Northwest Christian College	Eugene, OR	Crusaders
Northwest College	Kirkland, WA	Eagles
Northwest Missouri State University	Maryville, MO	Bearcats
Northwest Nazarene College	Nampa, ID	Crusaders
Northwestern College	Orange City, IA	Red Raiders
Northwestern College	St. Paul, MN	Eagles
Northwestern Oklahoma State University	Alva, OK	Rangers
Northwestern State University	Natchitoches, LA	Demons
Northwestern University	Evanston, IL	Wildcats
Northwood University	W. Palm Beach, FL	Seahawks
Northwood University	Midland, MI	Timberwolves
Northwood University	Cedar Hill, TX	Knights
Norwich University	Northfield, VT	Cadets
Notre Dame College	Manchester, NH	Saints
Notre Dame College	South Euclid, OH	Blue Falcons
Notre Dame de Namur University	Belmont, CA	Argonauts
Notre Dame of MD (Women), College of	Baltimore, MD	Gators
Notre Dame University	South Bend, IN	Fighting Irish
Nova Southeastern University	Davie, FL	Knights
Nyack College	Nyack, NY	Purple Pride

O

Institution Name	Location	Nickname/Mascot
Oak Hills Christian College	Bemidji, MN	Wolfpack
Oakland University	Rochester, MI	Golden Grizzlies
Oakland City University	Oakland City, IN	Mighty Oaks
Oberlin College	Oberlin, OH	Yeomen
Occidental College	Los Angeles, CA	Tigers
Oglala Lakota College	Kyle, SD	Brave Hearts
Oglethorpe University	Atlanta, GA	Stormy Petrels
Ohio Dominican College	Columbus, OH	Panthers
Ohio Northern University	Ada, OH	Polar Bears
Ohio State University	Columbus, OH	Buckeyes
Ohio University	Athens, OH	Bobcats
Ohio Valley College	Parkersburg, WV	Fighting Scots
Ohio Wesleyan University	Delaware, OH	Battling Bishops

Senior Colleges and Universities—United States
Alphabetic Listing by Institution

Institution Name	Location	Nickname/Mascot
Oklahoma, University of	Norman, OK	Sooners
Oklahoma Baptist College & Institute	Oklahoma City, OK	Prophets
Oklahoma Baptist University	Shawnee, OK	Bison
Oklahoma Christian University	Oklahoma City, OK	Eagles
Oklahoma City University	Oklahoma City, OK	Stars
Oklahoma Panhandle State University	Goodwell, OK	Aggies
Oklahoma State University	Stillwater, OK	Cowboys
Oklahoma Wesleyan University	Bartlesville, OK	Eagles
Old Dominion University	Norfolk, VA	Monarchs
Olivet College	Olivet, MI	Comets
Olivet Nazarene University	Bourbonnais, IL	Tigers
Oral Roberts University	Tulsa, OK	Golden Eagles
Oregon, University of	Eugene, OR	Ducks
Oregon State University	Corvallis, OR	Beavers
Oregon Institute of Technology	Klamath Falls, OR	Hustlin' Owls
Ottawa University	Ottawa, KS	Braves
Otterbein College	Westerville, OH	Cardinals
Ouachita Baptist University	Arkadelphia, AR	Tigers
Our Lady of the Lake University	San Antonio, TX	Armadillos
Ozark Christian College	Joplin, MO	Ambassadors
Ozarks, College of the	Point Lookout, MO	Bobcats
Ozarks, University of the	Clarksville, AR	Eagles

P

Institution Name	Location	Nickname/Mascot
Pace University	Pleasantville, NY	Setters
Pacific, University of the	Stockton, CA	Tigers
Pacific Christian College	Fullerton, CA	Royals
Pacific Coast Baptist Bible College	San Dimas, CA	Eagles
Pacific Lutheran University	Tacoma, WA	Lutes
Pacific Union College	Angwin, CA	Pioneers
Pacific University	Forest Grove, OR	Boxers
Paine College	Augusta, GA	Lions
Palm Beach Atlantic College	W. Palm Beach, FL	Sailfish
Park University	Parkville, MO	Pirates
Parks College of St. Louis University	Cahokia, IL	Falcons
Patten College	Oakland, CA	Lions
Paul Quinn College	Dallas, TX	Tigers
Peace College (Women)	Raleigh, NC	Pride
Pembroke State University	Pembroke, NC	Braves
Pennsylvania, University of	Philadelphia, PA	Quakers
Pennsylvania College of Technology	Williamsport, PA	Wildcats

Senior Colleges and Universities—United States
Alphabetic Listing by Institution

Institution Name	Location	Nickname/Mascot
Penn State University	State College, PA	Nittany Lions
Penn State University–Abington	Abington, PA	Lions
Penn State University–Beaver	Monaca, PA	Nittany Lions
Penn State University–Berks/Lehigh Val.	Reading, PA	Nittany Lions
Penn State University–Delaware	Media, PA	Nittany Lions
Penn State University–DuBois	DuBois, PA	Dukes
Penn State University–Fayette	Uniontown, PA	Roaring Lions
Penn State University–Hazleton	Hazleton, PA	Nittany Lions
Penn State University–McKeesport	McKeesport, PA	Lions
Penn State University–Mont Alto	Mont Alto, PA	Lions
Penn State University–New Kensington	New Kensington,PA	Lions
Penn State University–Schuylkill	Schuylkill Haven,PA	Lions
Penn State University–Wilkes-Barre	Lehman, PA	Mountain Lions
Penn State University–Worthington/Scranton	Dunmore, PA	Nittany Lions
Penn State University–York	York, PA	Lions
Pensacola Christian College	Pensacola, FL	Eagles
Pepperdine University	Malibu, CA	Waves
Peru State College	Peru, NE	Bobcats
Pfeiffer University	Misenheimer, NC	Falcons
Philadelphia Biblical University	Langhorne, PA	Crimson Eagles
Philadelphia University	Philadelphia, PA	Rams
Philander Smith College	Little Rock, AR	Panthers
Piedmont College	Demorest, GA	Lions
Piedmont Baptist College	Winston-Salem, NC	Conquerors
Pikeville College	Pikeville, KY	Bears
Pillsbury Baptist Bible College	Owatonna, MN	Comets
Pine Manor College (Women)	Chestnut Hill, MA	Gators
Pittsburgh, University of	Pittsburgh, PA	Panthers
Pittsburgh–Bradford, University of	Bradford, PA	Panthers
Pittsburgh–Greensburg, University of	Greensburg, PA	Bobcats
Pittsburgh–Johnstown, University of	Johnstown, PA	Mountain Cats
Pittsburg State University	Pittsburg, KS	Gorillas
Plymouth State College	Plymouth, NH	Panthers
Point Loma Nazarene University	San Diego, CA	Crusaders
Point Park College	Pittsburgh, PA	Pioneers
Polytechnic University	Brooklyn, NY	Blue Jays
Pomona-Pitzer Colleges	Claremont, CA	Sagehens
Portland, University of	Portland, OR	Pilots
Portland State University	Portland, OR	Vikings
Practical Biblical College	Johnson City, NY	Swordsmen
Prairie View A & M University	Prairie View, TX	Panthers

Senior Colleges and Universities—United States
Alphabetic Listing by Institution

Institution Name	Location	Nickname/Mascot
Pratt Institute	Brooklyn, NY	Cannoneers
Presbyterian College	Clinton, SC	Blue Hose
Presentation College	Aberdeen, SD	Saints
Princeton University	Princeton, NJ	Tigers
Principia College	Elsah, IL	Panthers
Providence College	Providence, RI	Friars
Puget Sound, University of	Tacoma, WA	Loggers
Puget Sound Christian College	Edmonds, WA	Anchormen
Purdue University	West Lafayette, IN	Boilermakers
Purdue University–Calumet	Hammond, IN	Lakers
Purdue University–North Central	Westville, IN	Centaurs

Q

Queens College	Charlotte, NC	Royals
Queens College of CUNY	Flushing, NY	Knights
Quincy University	Quincy, IL	Hawks
Quinnipiac College	Hamden, CT	Bobcats

R

Radford University	Radford, VA	Highlanders
Ramapo College of New Jersey	Mahwah, NJ	Roadrunners
Randolph-Macon College	Ashland, VA	Yellow Jackets
Randolph-Macon Women's College	Lynchburg, VA	Wildcats
Redlands, University of	Redlands, CA	Bulldogs
Regis College (Women)	Weston, MA	Pride
Regis University	Denver, CO	Rangers
Reinhardt College	Waleska, GA	Eagles
Rensselaer Polytech Institute (RPI)	Troy, NY	Engineers/Red Hawks
Rhema Bible College	Broken Arrow, OK	Eagles
Rhode Island College	Providence, RI	Anchormen
Rhode Island, University of	Kingston, RI	Rams
Rhodes College	Memphis, TN	Lynx
Rice University	Houston, TX	Owls
Richard Stockton College of N.J.	Pomona, NJ	Ospreys
Richmond, University of	Richmond, VA	Spiders
Rider University	Lawrenceville, NJ	Broncs
Rio Grande, University of	Rio Grande, OH	Redmen
Ripon College	Ripon, WI	Red Hawks
Rivier College	Nashua, NH	Raiders
Roanoke College	Salem, VA	Maroons

Senior Colleges and Universities—United States
Alphabetic Listing by Institution

Institution Name	Location	Nickname/Mascot
Roanoke Bible College	Elizabeth City, NC	Flames
Robert Morris College	Coraopolis, PA	Colonials
Robert Morris College–Springfield	Springfield, IL	Eagles
Roberts Wesleyan College	Rochester, NY	Raiders
Rochester College	Rochester Hills, MI	Warriors
Rochester, University of	Rochester, NY	Yellowjackets
Rochester Institute of Technology (RIT)	Rochester, NY	Tigers
Rockford College	Rockford, IL	Regents
Rockhurst College	Kansas City, MO	Hawks
Rocky Mountain College	Billings, MT	Battlin' Bears
Roger Williams University	Bristol, RI	Hawks
Rollins College	Winter Park, FL	Tars
Roosevelt University	Chicago, IL	Lakers
Rose-Hulman Institute of Technology	Terre Haute, IN	Engineers
Rosemont College (Women)	Rosemont, PA	Ramblers
Russell Sage College (Women)	Troy, NY	Gators
Rowan University	Glassboro, NJ	Profs
Rust College	Holly Springs, MS	Bearcats
Rutgers University	New Brunswick, NJ	Scarlet Knights
Rutgers University–Camden	Camden, NJ	Scarlet Raptors
Rutgers University–Newark	Newark, NJ	Scarlet Raiders

S

Institution Name	Location	Nickname/Mascot
Sacred Heart University	Fairfield, CT	Pioneers
Saginaw Valley State University	University Center, MI	Cardinals
St. Ambrose University	Davenport, IA	Fighting Bees/Queen Bees
St. Andrew's Presbyterian College	Laurinburg, NC	Knights
St. Anselm College	Manchester, NH	Hawks
St. Augustine's College	Raleigh, NC	Falcons
St. Benedict (Women), College of	St. Joseph, MN	Blazers
St. Bonaventure University	St. Bonaventure, NY	Bonnies
St. Catherine (Women), College of	St. Paul, MN	Wildcats
St. Cloud State University	St. Cloud, MN	Huskies
St. Edward's University	Austin, TX	Hilltoppers
St. Elizabeth (Women), College of	Morristown, NJ	Eagles
St. Francis, University of	Joliet, IL	Fighting Saints
St. Francis, University of	Ft. Wayne, IN	Cougars
St. Francis College	Brooklyn Heights, NY	Terriers
St. Francis College	Loretto, PA	Red Flash
St. Gregory's University	Shawnee, OK	Cavaliers
St. John Fisher College	Rochester, NY	Cardinals

Senior Colleges and Universities—United States
Alphabetic Listing by Institution

Institution Name	Location	Nickname/Mascot
St. John's University	Collegeville, MN	Johnnies
St. John's University	Jamaica, NY	Red Storm
St. Joseph College (Women)	West Hartford,CT	Blue Jays
St. Joseph in Vermont, College of	Rutland, VT	Fighting Saints
St. Joseph's College	Brooklyn, NY	Bears
St. Joseph's College	Rensselaer, IN	Pumas
St. Joseph's College of Maine	Standish, ME	Monks
St. Joseph's College—Suffolk	Patchogue, LI, NY	Golden Eagles
St. Joseph's University	Philadelphia, PA	Hawks
St. Lawrence University	Canton, NY	Saints
St. Leo University	St. Leo, FL	Lions
St. Louis Christian College	Florissant, MO	Soldiers
St. Louis College of Pharmacy	St. Louis, MO	Eutectics
St. Louis University	St. Louis, MO	Billikens
St. Martin's College	Lacey, WA	Saints
St. Mary (Women), College of	Omaha, NE	Flames
St. Mary College	Leavenworth, KS	Spires
St. Mary-of-the-Woods College (Women)	St. Mary—OTW, IN	Pomeroys
St. Mary's College of Ave Maria University	Orchard Lake, MI	Eagles
St. Mary's Col. of Notre Dame University	Notre Dame, IN	Belles
St. Mary's College of California	Moraga, CA	Gaels
St. Mary's College of Maryland	St. Mary's City, MD	Seahawks
St. Mary's University	San Antonio, TX	Rattlers
St. Mary's University of Minnesota	Winona, MN	Cardinals
St. Michael's College	Colchester, VT	Purple Knights
St. Norbert College	De Pere, WI	Green Knights
St. Olaf College	Northfield, MN	Oles or Lions
St. Paul's College	Lawrenceville, VA	Tigers
St. Peter's College	Jersey City, NJ	Peacocks/Peahens
St. Rose, College of	Albany, NY	Golden Knights
St. Scholastica, College of	Duluth, MN	Saints
St. Thomas, University of	Houston, TX	Celts
St. Thomas, University of	St. Paul, MN	Tommies
St. Thomas University	Miami, FL	Bobcats
St. Thomas Aquinas College	Sparkill, NY	Spartans
St. Vincent College	Latrobe, PA	Bearcats
St. Xavier University	Chicago, IL	Cougars
Salem College (Women)	Winston-Salem, NC	Spirits
Salem State College	Salem, MA	Vikings
Salem-Teikyo University	Salem, WV	Tigers
Salisbury University	Salisbury, MD	Sea Gulls
Salve Regina College	Newport, RI	Seahawks

Senior Colleges and Universities—United States
Alphabetic Listing by Institution

Institution Name	Location	Nickname/Mascot
Sam Houston State University	Huntsville, TX	Bearkats
Samford University	Birmingham, AL	Bulldogs
San Diego, University of	San Diego, CA	Toreros
San Francisco, University of	San Francisco, CA	Dons
San Francisco State University	San Francisco, CA	Gators
San Jose Christian College	San Jose, CA	Warriors
Santa Clara University	Santa Clara, CA	Broncos
Santa Fe, College of	Santa Fe, NM	Knights
Sarah Lawrence College	Bronxville, NY	Gryphons
Savannah College of Art & Design	Savannah, GA	Bees
Savannah State University	Savannah, GA	Tigers
Schreiner College	Kerrville, TX	Mountaineers
Science & Arts of Oklahoma, University of	Chickasha, OK	Drovers
Sciences in Philadelphia, University of the	Philadelphia, PA	Blue Devils
Scranton, University of	Scranton, PA	Royals
Seattle University	Seattle, WA	Redhawks
Seattle Pacific University	Seattle, WA	Falcons
Selma University	Selma, AL	Bulldogs
Seton Hall University	South Orange, NJ	Pirates
Seton Hill College	Greensburg, PA	Spirit, The
Shaw University	Raleigh, NC	Bears
Shawnee State University	Portsmouth, OH	Bears
Shenandoah University	Winchester, VA	Hornets
Shepherd College	Shepherdstown, WV	Rams
Shippensburg University	Shippensburg, PA	Red Raiders
Shorter College	Rome, GA	Hawks
Siena College	Loudonville, NY	Saints
Siena Heights College	Adrian, MI	Saints
Sierra Nevada College	Incline Village, NV	Eagles
Silver Lake College	Manitowoc, WI	Lakers
Simmons College (Women)	Boston, MA	Sharks
Simpson College	Indianola, IA	Storm
Simpson College	Redding, CA	Vanguards
Simpson College	San Francisco, CA	Knights
Sioux Falls, University of	Sioux Falls, SD	Cougars
Skidmore College	Saratoga, NY	Thoroughbreds
Smith College (Women)	Northampton, MA	Pioneers
Slippery Rock University	Slippery Rock, PA	Rock, The
Sonoma State University	Rohnert Park, CA	Cossacks
South, University of the	Sewanee, TN	Tigers
South Alabama, University of	Mobile, AL	Jaguars
South Carolina, University of	Columbia, SC	Gamecocks

Senior Colleges and Universities—United States
Alphabetic Listing by Institution

Institution Name	Location	Nickname/Mascot
South Carolina–Aiken, University of	Aiken, SC	Pacers
South Carolina–Spartanburg, University of	Spartanburg, SC	Rifles
South Carolina State College	Orangeburg, SC	Bulldogs
South Dakota, University of	Vermillion, SD	Coyotes
South Dakota State University	Brookings, SD	Jackrabbits
South Dakota School of Mines & Technology	Rapid City, SD	Hardrockers
South Florida, University of	Tampa, FL	Bulls
Southeast Missouri State University	Cape Giradeau, MO	Indians or Otahkians
Southeastern University	Washington, DC	Hawks
Southeastern College	Lakeland, FL	Crusaders
Southeastern Baptist College	Laurel, MS	Chargers
Southeastern Bible College	Birmingham, AL	Sabers
Southeastern Louisiana University	Hammond, LA	Lions
Southeastern Massachusetts University	North Dartmouth, MA	Corsairs
Southeastern Oklahoma State University	Durant, OK	Savages
Southern Arkansas University	Magnolia, AR	Muleriders
Southern Baptist College	Walnut Ridge, AR	Eagles
Southern Bible College	Houston, TX	Lions
Southern California, University of (USC)	Los Angeles, CA	Trojans/Women of Troy
Southern Christian University	Jacksonville, FL	Bears
Southern Colorado, University of	Pueblo, CO	Thunderwolves
Southern Connecticut State University	New Haven, CT	Owls
Southern Idaho, College of	Twin Falls, ID	Golden Eagles
Southern Illinois University–Carbondale	Carbondale, IL	Salukis
Southern Illinois University–Edwardsville	Edwardsville, IL	Cougars
Southern Indiana, University of	Evansville, IN	Screaming Eagles
Southern Maine, University of	Gorham, ME	Huskies
Southern Methodist University	Dallas, TX	Mustangs
Southern Mississippi, University of	Hattiesburg, MS	Golden Eagles
Southern Nazarene University	Bethany, OK	Crimson Storm
Southern Oregon University	Ashland, OR	Raiders
Southern Poly State University	Marietta, GA	Hornets
Southern University and A&M College	Baton Rouge, LA	Jaguars
Southern University at New Orleans	New Orleans, LA	Knights
Southern Utah University	Cedar City, UT	Thunderbirds
Southern Virginia University	Buena Vista, VA	Knights
Southern Vermont College	Bennington, VT	Mountaineers
Southern Wesleyan University	Central, SC	Warriors
Southwest, College of the	Hobbs, NM	Mustangs
Southwest Baptist University	Bolivar, MO	Bearcats
Southwest Missouri State University	Springfield, MO	Bears
Southwest State University	Marshall, MN	Mustangs

Senior Colleges and Universities—United States
Alphabetic Listing by Institution

Institution Name	Location	Nickname/Mascot
Southwest Texas State University	San Marcos, TX	Bobcats
Southwestern Adventist University	Keene, TX	Knights
Southwestern Assemblies of God University	Waxahachie, TX	Lions
Southwestern Christian University	Bethany, OK	Eagles
Southwestern College	Phoenix, AZ	Eagles
Southwestern College	Winfield, KS	Moundbuilders
Southwestern Oklahoma State University	Weatherford, OK	Bulldogs
Southwestern University	Georgetown, TX	Pirates
Spalding University	Louisville, KY	Pelicans
Spelman College (Women)	Atlanta, GA	Jaguars
Spring Arbor University	Spring Arbor, MI	Cougars
Spring Hill College	Mobile, AL	Badgers
Springfield College	Springfield, MA	Pride
Stanford University	Palo Alto, CA	Cardinal
Staten Island of CUNY, College of	Staten Island, NY	Dolphins
Stephen F. Austin State University	Nacogdoches, TX	Lumberjacks/Ladyjacks
Stephens College (Women)	Columbia, MO	Stars
Sterling College	Sterling, KS	Warriors
Stetson University	Deland, FL	Hatters
Steubenville University	Steubenville, OH	Saints
Stevens Institute of Technology	Hoboken, NJ	Ducks
Stillman College	Tuscaloosa, AL	Tigers
Stonehill College	North Easton, MA	Chieftains
Strayer University	Washington, DC	Tigers
Suffolk University	Boston, MA	Rams
Sul Ross State University	Alpine, TX	Lobos
SUNY—Albany	Albany, NY	Great Danes
SUNY—Binghamton	Binghamton, NY	Bearcats
SUNY—Brockport	Brockport, NY	Golden Eagles
SUNY—Buffalo	Buffalo, NY	Bulls
SUNY—Buffalo State College	Buffalo, NY	Bengals
SUNY—Cortland	Cortland, NY	Red Dragons
SUNY—Farmingdale	Farmingdale, NY	Rams
SUNY—Fashion Institute of Technology	New York, NY	Tigers
SUNY—Fredonia	Fredonia, NY	Blue Devils
SUNY—Geneseo	Geneseo, NY	Blue Knights
SUNY—Institute of Tech. at Utica/Rome	Utica, NY	Wildcats
SUNY—New Paltz	New Paltz, NY	Hawks
SUNY—New York Maritime College	Ft. Schuyler, NY	Privateers
SUNY—Old Westbury	Old Westbury, NY	Panthers
SUNY—Oneonta	Oneonta, NY	Red Dragons
SUNY—Oswego	Oswego, NY	Lakers
SUNY—Plattsburgh	Plattsburgh, NY	Cardinals

Senior Colleges and Universities—United States
Alphabetic Listing by Institution

Institution Name	Location	Nickname/Mascot
SUNY–Potsdam	Potsdam, NY	Bears
SUNY–Purchase College	Purchase, NY	Panthers
SUNY–Stony Brook	Stony Brook, NY	Seawolves
Susquehanna University	Selinsgrove, PA	Crusaders
Swarthmore College	Swarthmore, PA	Garnet Tide
Sweet Briar College (Women)	Sweet Briar, VA	Vixens
Syracuse University	Syracuse, NY	Orangemen

T

Institution Name	Location	Nickname/Mascot
Tabor College	Hillsboro, KS	Bluejays
Talladega College	Talladega, AL	Tornados
Tampa, University of	Tampa, FL	Spartans
Tarleton State University	Stephenville, TX	Texans
Taylor University	Upland, IN	Trojans
Taylor University–Ft. Wayne	Ft. Wayne, IN	Falcons
Teikyo Post University	Waterbury, CT	Eagles
Temple Baptist College	Cincinnati, OH	Rams
Temple University	Philadelphia, PA	Owls
Tennessee, University of	Knoxville, TN	Volunteers
Tennessee–Chattanooga, University of	Chattanooga, TN	Mocs
Tennessee–Martin, University of	Martin, TN	Skyhawks
Tennessee State University	Nashville, TN	Tigers
Tennessee Technical University	Cookeville, TN	Golden Eagles
Tennessee Temple University	Chattanooga, TN	Crusaders
Tennessee Wesleyan College	Athens, TN	Bulldogs
Texas, University of	Austin, TX	Longhorns
Texas–Arlington, University of	Arlington, TX	Mavericks
Texas–Brownsville, University of and Texas Southmost College	Brownsville, TX	Scorpions
Texas–Dallas, University of	Richardson, TX	Comets
Texas–El Paso, University of (UTEP)	El Paso, TX	Miners
Texas–Pan American, University of	Edinburg, TX	Broncs
Texas–Permian Basin, University of	Odessa, TX	Falcons
Texas–San Antonio, University of	San Antonio, TX	Roadrunners
Texas–Tyler, University of	Tyler, TX	Patriots
Texas A&M University	College Station, TX	Aggies
Texas A&M University–Commerce	Commerce, TX	Lions
Texas A&M University–Corpus Christi	Corpus Christi, TX	Islanders
Texas A&M University–Kingsville	Kingsville, TX	Javelinas
Texas Christian University (TCU)	Ft. Worth, TX	Horned Frogs
Texas College	Tyler, TX	Steers
Texas Lutheran University	Seguin, TX	Bulldogs

Senior Colleges and Universities—United States
Alphabetic Listing by Institution

Institution Name	Location	Nickname/Mascot
Texas Southern University	Houston, TX	Tigers
Texas Technical University	Lubbock, TX	Red Raiders
Texas Wesleyan University	Ft. Worth, TX	Rams
Texas Women's University	Denton, TX	Pioneers
Thiel College	Greenville, PA	Tomcats/Lady Cats
Thomas College	Waterville, ME	Terriers
Thomas University	Thomasville, GA	Night Hawks
Thomas More College	Crestview Hills, KY	Saints
Tiffin University	Tiffin, OH	Dragons
Toccoa Falls College	Toccoa Falls, GA	Eagles
Toledo, University of	Toledo, OH	Rockets
Tougaloo College	Tougaloo, MS	Bulldogs
Towson State University	Towson, MD	Tigers
Transylvania University	Lexington, KY	Pioneers
Trevecca Nazarene University	Nashville, TN	Trojans
Tri-State University	Angola, IN	Thunder
Trinity Baptist College	Jacksonville, FL	Eagles
Trinity Bible College	Ellendale, ND	Lions
Trinity Christian College	Palos Heights, IL	Trolls
Trinity College	Hartford, CT	Bantams
Trinity College (Women)	Washington, DC	Tigers
Trinity College of Florida	New Port Richey, FL	Tigers
Trinity International University	Deerfield, IL	Trojans
Trinity University	San Antonio, TX	Tigers
Troy State University	Troy, AL	Trojans
Truman State University	Kirksville, MO	Bulldogs
Tufts University	Medford, MA	Jumbos
Tulane University	New Orleans, LA	Green Wave
Tulsa, University of	Tulsa, OK	Golden Hurricanes
Tusculum College	Greenville, TN	Pioneers
Tuskegee University	Tuskegee, AL	Golden Tigers

U

Institution Name	Location	Nickname/Mascot
Union College	Barbourville, KY	Bulldogs
Union College	Lincoln, NE	Warriors
Union College	Schenectady, NY	Dutchmen
Union University	Jackson, TN	Bulldogs
U.S. Air Force Academy	Colorado Springs, CO	Falcons
U.S. Coast Guard Academy	New London, CT	Bears
U.S. Marine Corps Academy	Quantico, VA	Marines
U.S. Merchant Marine Academy	Kings Point, NY	Mariners

Senior Colleges and Universities—United States
Alphabetic Listing by Institution

Institution Name	Location	Nickname/Mascot
U.S. Military Academy	West Point, NY	Cadets or Black Knights
U.S. Naval Academy	Annapolis, MD	Midshipmen
United Wesleyan College	Allentown, PA	Warriors
Unity College	Unity, ME	Rams
Upper Iowa University	Fayette, IA	Peacocks
Urbana University	Urbana, OH	Blue Knights
Ursinus College	Collegeville, PA	Bears
Ursuline College (Women)	Pepper Pike, OH	Arrows
Utah, University of	Salt Lake City, UT	Utes
Utah State University	Logan, UT	Aggies
Utah Valley State College	Orem, UT	Wolverines
Utica College of Syracuse University	Utica, NY	Pioneers

V

Institution Name	Location	Nickname/Mascot
Valdosta State University	Valdosta, GA	Blazers
Valley City State University	Valley City, ND	Vikings
Valley Forge Christian College	Phoenixville, PA	Patriots
Valparaiso University	Valparaiso, IN	Crusaders
Vanderbilt University	Nashville, TN	Commodores
Vanguard University of Southern Cal.	Costa Mesa, CA	Lions
Vassar College	Poughkeepsie, NY	Brewers
Vennard College	University Park, IA	Cougars
Vermont, University of	Burlington, VT	Catamounts
Vermont Technical College	Randolph Center, VT	Green Knights
Villa Julie College	Stevenson, MD	Mustangs
Villa Maria College	Erie, PA	Crusaders
Villanova University	Villanova, PA	Wildcats
Virgin Islands, University of the	St. Thomas, VI	Buccaneers
Virginia, University of	Charlottesville, VA	Cavaliers
Virginia Commonwealth University	Richmond, VA	Rams
Virginia Intermont College	Bristol, VA	Cobras
Virginia Military Institute (VMI)	Lexington, VA	Keydets
Virginia Polytechnic Institute and State University (Virginia Tech)	Blacksburg, VA	Hokies or Gobblers
Virginia State University	Petersburg, VA	Trojans
Virginia Union University	Richmond, VA	Panthers
Virginia Wesleyan College	Norfolk, VA	Blue Marlins
Virginia-Wise, University of	Wise, VA	Highland Cavaliers
Viterbo College	La Crosse, WI	V-Hawks
Voorhees College	Denmark, SC	Tigers

Senior Colleges and Universities—United States
Alphabetic Listing by Institution

Institution Name	Location	Nickname/Mascot

W

Institution Name	Location	Nickname/Mascot
Wabash College	Crawfordsville, IN	Little Giants
Wagner College	Staten Island, NY	Seahawks
Wake Forest University	Winston-Salem, NC	Demon Deacons
Waldorf College	Forest City, IA	Warriors
Walla Walla College	College Place, WA	Wolves
Walsh University	Canton, OH	Cavaliers
Warner Pacific College	Portland, OR	Knights
Warner Southern College	Lake Wales, FL	Royals
Warren-Wilson College	Swannanoa, NC	Owls
Wartburg College	Waverly, IA	Knights
Washburn University	Topeka, KS	Ichabods/Lady Blues
Washington, University of	Seattle, WA	Huskies
Washington & Jefferson College	Washington, PA	Presidents
Washington & Lee University	Lexington, VA	Generals
Washington Bible College	Lanham, MD	Cougars
Washington College	Chestertown, MD	Shoremen
Washington State University	Pullman, WA	Cougars
Washington University	St. Louis, MO	Bears
Wayland Baptist University	Plainview, TX	Pioneers/Flying Queens
Wayne State College	Wayne, NE	Wildcats
Wayne State University	Detroit, MI	Warriors
Waynesburg College	Waynesburg, PA	Yellowjackets
Webb Institute	Glen Cove, LI, NY	Clippers
Webber College	Babson Park, FL	Warriors
Weber State University	Ogden, UT	Wildcats
Webster University	Webster Groves, MO	Gorloks
Wellesley College (Women)	Wellesley, MA	Blue, The
Wells College (Women)	Aurora, NY	Express, The
Wentworth Institute of Technology	Boston, MA	Leopards
Wesley College	Dover, DE	Wolverines
Wesleyan College (Women)	Macon, GA	Pioneers
Wesleyan University	Middletown, CT	Cardinals
West Alabama, University of	Livingston, AL	Tigers
West Chester University of Pennsylvania	West Chester, PA	Golden Rams
West Florida, University of	Pensacola, FL	Argonauts
West Georgia, State University of	Carrollton, GA	Braves
West Liberty State College	West Liberty, WV	Hilltoppers
West Texas A&M University	Canyon, TX	Buffaloes
West Virginia, University of	Morgantown, WV	Mountaineers
West Virginia State College	Institute, WV	Yellow Jackets

Senior Colleges and Universities—United States
Alphabetic Listing by Institution

Institution Name	Location	Nickname/Mascot
West Virginia University Institute of Tech.	Montgomery, WV	Golden Bears
West Virginia Wesleyan College	Buckhannon, WV	Bobcats
Western Baptist College	Salem, OR	Warriors
Western Carolina University	Cullowhee, NC	Catamounts
Western Connecticut State University	Danbury, CT	Colonials
Western Illinois University	Macomb, IL	Leathernecks/Westerwinds
Western Kentucky University	Bowling Green, KY	Hilltoppers
Western Michigan University	Kalamazoo, MI	Broncos
Western New England College	Springfield, MA	Golden Bears
Western New Mexico University	Silver City, NM	Mustangs
Western Oregon University	Monmouth, OR	Wolves
Western State College of Colorado	Gunnison, CO	Mountaineers
Western Washington University	Bellingham, WA	Vikings
Westfield State College	Westfield, MA	Owls
Westminster College	Fulton, MO	Blue Jays
Westminster College	New Wilmington, PA	Titans
Westminster College	Salt Lake City, UT	Griffins
Westmont College	Santa Barbara, CA	Warriors
Wheaton College	Norton, MA	Lyons
Wheaton College	Wheaton, IL	Thunder
Wheeling Jesuit University	Wheeling, WV	Cardinals
Wheelock College	Boston, MA	Wildcats
Whitman College	Walla Walla, WA	Missionaries
Whittier College	Whittier, CA	Poets
Whitworth College	Spokane, WA	Pirates
Wichita State University	Wichita, KS	Shockers
Widener University	Chester, PA	Pioneers
Wilberforce University	Wilberforce, OH	Bulldogs
Wiley College	Marshall, TX	Wildcats
Wilkes University	Wilkes-Barre, PA	Colonels
Willamette University	Salem, OR	Bearcats
William & Mary, College of	Williamsburg, VA	Tribe
William Carey College	Hattiesburg, MS	Crusaders
William Jewell College	Liberty, MO	Cardinals
William Paterson University	Wayne, NJ	Pioneers
William Penn University	Oskaloosa, IA	Statesmen
William Smith College	Geneva, NY	Herons
William Tyndale College	Farmington Hills, MI	Lancers
William Woods University	Fulton, MO	Owls
Williams College	Williamstown, MA	Ephmen/Ephwomen
Williams Baptist College	Walnut Ridge, AR	Eagles
Wilmington College	New Castle, DE	Wildcats

Senior Colleges and Universities—United States
Alphabetic Listing by Institution

Institution Name	Location	Nickname/Mascot
Wilmington College	Wilmington, OH	Quakers
Wilson College (Women)	Chambersburg, PA	Phoenix
Wingate University	Wingate, NC	Bulldogs
Winona State University	Winona, MN	Warriors
Winston-Salem State University	Winston-Salem, NC	Rams
Winthrop University	Rock Hill, SC	Eagles
Wisconsin, University of	Madison, WI	Badgers
Wisconsin—Eau Claire, University of	Eau Claire, WI	Blugolds
Wisconsin—Green Bay, University of	Green Bay, WI	Phoenix
Wisconsin—LaCrosse, University of	LaCrosse, WI	Eagles
Wisconsin—Milwaukee, University of	Milwaukee, WI	Panthers
Wisconsin—Oshkosh, University of	Oshkosh, WI	Titans
Wisconsin—Parkside, University of	Kenosha, WI	Rangers
Wisconsin—Platteville, University of	Platteville, WI	Pioneers
Wisconsin—River Falls, University of	River Falls, WI	Falcons
Wisconsin—Stevens Point, University of	Stevens Point, WI	Pointers
Wisconsin—Stout, University of	Menomonie, WI	Blue Devils
Wisconsin—Superior, University of	Superior, WI	Yellowjackets
Wisconsin—Whitewater, University of	Whitewater, WI	Warhawks
Wisconsin Lutheran College	Milwaukee, WI	Warriors
Wittenberg University	Springfield, OH	Tigers
Wofford College	Spartanburg, SC	Terriers
Wooster, College of	Wooster, OH	Fighting Scots
Worcester Polytechnic Institute	Worcester, MA	Engineers
Worcester State College	Worcester, MA	Lancers
World Harvest Bible College	Columbus, OH	Warriors
Wright State University	Dayton, OH	Raiders
Wyoming, University of	Laramie, WY	Cowboys/Cowgirls

X

Xavier University	Cincinnati, OH	Musketeers
Xavier University of Louisiana	New Orleans, LA	Gold Rush/Nuggets

Y

Yale University	New Haven, CT	Bulldogs
Yeshiva University	New York, NY	Maccabees
York College of CUNY	Jamaica, NY	Cardinals
York College	York, NE	Panthers
York College of Pennsylvania	York, PA	Spartans
Youngstown State University	Youngstown, OH	Penguins

Part 2

Senior Colleges and Universities

United States

Alphabetic Listing by Nickname / Mascot

Did you know. . .

nick•name, n. a name added to or substituted for the proper name of a person, place, etc., as in ridicule or familiarity.

Random House Dictionary
of the English Language

that Wake Forest University is the second-smallest school in the country to field teams in 1-A athletics. The undergraduate population is approximately 4,100. Do you know who is the smallest? Hint: they are located in Staten Island, New York.

Senior Colleges and Universities—United States
Alphabetic Listing by Nickname/Mascot

Nickname/Mascot	Institution Name	Location

A

49ers	Cal State University—Long Beach State	Long Beach, CA
49ers	North Carolina—Charlotte, University of	Charlotte, NC
Aggies	Cal—Davis, University of	Davis, CA
Aggies	Cameron University	Lawton, OK
Aggies	Delaware Valley College	Doylestown, PA
Aggies	New Mexico State University	Las Cruces, NM
Aggies	North Carolina A & T State University	Greensboro, NC
Aggies	Oklahoma Panhandle State University	Goodwell, OK
Aggies	Texas A & M University	College Station, TX
Aggies	Utah State University	Logan, UT
All-Stars	Converse College (Women)	Spartanburg, SC
Ambassadors	Multnomah Bible College	Portland, OR
Ambassadors	Oakwood College	Huntsville, AL
Ambassadors	Ozark Christian College	Joplin, MO
AMcats	Anna Maria College	Paxton, MA
Anchormen	Puget Sound Christian College	Edmonds, WA
Anchormen	Rhode Island College	Providence, RI
Angels	Meredith College	Raleigh, NC
Anteaters	Cal—Irvine, University of	Irvine, CA
Antelopes	Grand Canyon University	Phoenix, AZ
Antelopes	Nebraska—Kearney, University of	Kearney, NE
Archers	Moody Bible Institute	Chicago, IL
Argonauts	Great Falls, University of	Great Falls, MT
Argonauts	Notre Dame de Namur University	Belmont, CA
Argonauts	West Florida, University of	Pensacola, FL
Armadillos	Our Lady of the Lake University	San Antonio, TX
Arrows	Ursuline College (Women)	Pepper Pike, OH
Athenians	Mt. St. Mary's College (Women)	Los Angeles, CA
Auggies	Augsburg College	Minneapolis, MN
Aztecs	Cal State University—San Diego State	San Diego, CA

B

Badgers	Johnson State College	Johnson, VT
Badgers	Spring Hill College	Mobile, AL
Badgers	Wisconsin, University of	Madison, WI
Bald Eagles	Lock Haven University of Pennsylvania	Lock Haven, PA
Bald Eagles	McCoy College	West Hills, CA
Banana Slugs	Cal—Santa Cruz, University of	Santa Cruz, CA

Alphabetic Listing by Nickname/Mascot

Nickname/Mascot	Institution Name	Location
Bantams	Trinity College	Hartford, CT
Battlers	Alderson-Broaddus College	Philippi, WV
Battlin' Bears	Rocky Mountain College	Billings, MT
Battlin' Beavers	Blackburn College	Carlinville, IL
Battling Bishops	North Carolina Wesleyan College	Rocky Mount, NC
Battling Bishops	Ohio Wesleyan University	Delaware, OH
Beacons	Massachusetts—Boston, University of	Boston, MA
Bearcats	Brescia College	Owensboro, KY
Bearcats	Cincinnati, University of	Cincinnati, OH
Bearcats	McKendree College	Lebanon, IL
Bearcats	Northwest Missouri State University	Maryville, MO
Bearcats	Rust College	Holly Springs, MS
Bearcats	Southwest Baptist University	Bolivar, MO
Bearcats	St. Vincent College	Latrobe, PA
Bearcats	SUNY—Binghamton	Binghamton, NY
Bearcats	Willamette University	Salem, OR
Bearkats	Sam Houston State University	Huntsville, TX
Bears	Athens State University	Athens, AL
Bears	Barclay College	Haviland, KS
Bears	Baylor University	Waco, TX
Bears	Bridgewater State College	Bridgewater, MA
Bears	Brown University	Providence, RI
Bears	Central Arkansas, University of	Conway, AR
Bears	Golden State Baptist College	Santa Clara, CA
Bears	Lenoir-Rhyne College	Hickory, NC
Bears	Mercer University	Macon, GA
Bears	New York Institute of Technology	Old Westbury, NY
Bears	Northern Colorado, University of	Greeley, CO
Bears	Pikeville College	Pikeville, KY
Bears	Shaw University	Raleigh, NC
Bears	Shawnee State University	Portsmouth, OH
Bears	Southern Christian University	Jacksonville, FL
Bears	Southwest Missouri State University	Springfield, MO
Bears	St. Joseph's College	Brooklyn, NY
Bears	SUNY—Potsdam	Potsdam, NY
Bears	Ursinus College	Collegeville, PA
Bears	U.S. Coast Guard Academy	New London, CT
Bears	Washington University	St. Louis, MO
Beavers	Babson College	Babson Park, MA
Beavers	Bemidji State University	Bemidji, MN

Senior Colleges and Universities—United States
Alphabetic Listing by Nickname/Mascot

Nickname/Mascot	Institution Name	Location
Beavers	Bluffton College	Bluffton, OH
Beavers	Buena Vista University	Storm Lake, IA
Beavers	California Institute of Technology	Pasadena, CA
Beavers	Champlain College	Burlington, VT
Beavers	City College of New York (CCNY) of CUNY	New York, NY
Beavers	Maine–Farmington, University of	Farmington, ME
Beavers	Minot State University	Minot, ND
Beavers	Oregon State University	Corvallis, OR
Bees	Savannah College of Art & Design	Savannah, GA
Belles	St. Mary's College of Notre Dame University	Notre Dame, IN
Belles	Bennett College	Greensboro, NC
Bengals	Idaho State University	Pocatello, ID
Bengals	Maine–Fort Kent, University of	Fort Kent, ME
Bengals	SUNY–Buffalo State College	Buffalo, NY
Berg, The	Heidelberg College	Tiffin, OH
Big Blue	Millikin University	Decatur, IL
Big Blues	Bluefield State College	Bluefield, WV
Big Green	Dartmouth College	Hanover, NH
Big Red	Cornell University	Ithaca, NY
Big Red	Denison University	Granville, OH
Billikens	St. Louis University	St. Louis, MO
Bison	Bethany College	Bethany, WV
Bison	Bucknell University	Lewisburg, PA
Bison	Gallaudet University	Washington, DC
Bison	Harding University	Searcy, AR
Bison	Howard University	Washington, DC
Bison	Lipscomb University	Nashville, TN
Bison	Nichols College	Dudley, MA
Bison	North Dakota State University	Fargo, ND
Bison	Oklahoma Baptist University	Shawnee, OK
Black Bears	Maine, University of	Orono, ME
Blackbirds	Long Island University	Greenvale, NY
Blackbirds	Long Island University–Brooklyn Campus	Brooklyn, NY
Black Flies	Atlantic, College of the	Bar Harbor, ME
Blaze	Berkeley College	New York, NY
Blazers	Alabama–Birmingham, University of	Birmingham, AL
Blazers	Bard College	Annandale-on-Hudson, NY
Blazers	Belhaven College	Jackson, MS
Blazers	Elms College	Chicopee, MA
Blazers	Hood College	Frederick, MD
Blazers	St.Benedict (Women), College of	St. Joseph, MN

Senior Colleges and Universities—United States

Alphabetic Listing by Nickname/Mascot

Nickname/Mascot	Institution Name	Location
Blazers	Valdosta State University	Valdosta, GA
Bloodhounds	John Jay College of Criminal Justice of CUNY	New York, NY
Blue, The	Wellesley College (Women)	Wellesley, MA
Blue Angels	New Rochelle (Women), College of	New Rochelle, NY
Blue Bears	Livingstone College	Salisbury, NC
Blue Demons	DePaul University	Chicago, IL
Blue Devils	Duke University	Durham, NC
Blue Devils	Central Connecticut State University	New Britain, CT
Blue Devils	Dillard University	New Orleans, LA
Blue Devils	Lawrence Technical University	Southfield, MI
Blue Devils	Sciences in Phila., University of the	Philadelphia, PA
Blue Devils	SUNY—Fredonia	Fredonia, NY
Blue Devils	Wisconsin—Stout, University of	Menomonie, WI
Blue Falcons	Notre Dame College	South Euclid, OH
Blue Hawks	Dickinson State University	Dickinson, ND
Blue Hose	Presbyterian College	Clinton, SC
Blue Jays	Elizabethtown College	Elizabethtown, PA
Blue Jays	Johns Hopkins University	Baltimore, MD
Blue Jays	Polytechnic University	Brooklyn, NY
Blue Jays	St. Joseph College (Women)	West Hartford, NY
Blue Jays	Westminster College	Fulton, MO
Bluejays	Creighton University	Omaha, NE
Bluejays	Elmhurst College	Elmhurst, IL
Bluejays	Tabor College	Hillsboro, KS
Blue Knights	SUNY—Geneseo	Geneseo, NY
Blue Knights	Urbana University	Urbana, OH
Blue Marlins	Virginia Wesleyan College	Norfolk, VA
Blue Raiders	Lindsey Wilson College	Columbia, KY
Blue Raiders	Middle Tennessee State University	Murfreesboro, TN
Blue Streaks	John Carroll University	Cleveland, OH
Blue Tigers	Lincoln University	Jefferson City, MO
Blueboys/Lady Blues	Illinois College	Jacksonville, IL
Blues	Mississippi University for Women	Columbus, MS
Blugolds	Wisconsin—Eau Claire, University of	Eau Claire, WI
Bobcats	Bates College	Lewiston, ME
Bobcats	Frostburg State University	Frostburg, MD
Bobcats	Lees-McRae College	Banner Elk, NC
Bobcats	Montana State University—Bozeman	Bozeman, MT
Bobcats	Ohio University	Athens, OH
Bobcats	Ozarks, College of the	Point Lookout, MO
Bobcats	Peru State College	Peru, NE
Bobcats	Pittsburgh—Greensburg, University of	Greensburg, PA

Senior Colleges and Universities—United States
Alphabetic Listing by Nickname/Mascot

Nickname/Mascot	Institution Name	Location
Bobcats	Quinnipiac University	Hamden, CT
Bobcats	Southwest Texas State University	San Marcos, TX
Bobcats	St. Thomas University	Miami, FL
Bobcats	West Virginia Wesleyan College	Buckhannon, WV
Boilermakers	Purdue University	West Lafayette, IN
Boll Weevils/Cotton Blossoms	Arkansas–Monticello, University of	Monticello, AR
Bombers	Ithaca College	Ithaca, NY
Bonnies	St. Bonaventure University	St. Bonaventure, NY
Boxers	Pacific University	Forest Grove, OR
Brave Hearts	Oglala Lakota College	Kyle, SD
Braves	Alcorn State University	Lorman, MS
Braves	Bradley University	Peoria, IL
Braves	Chowan College	Murfreesboro, NC
Braves	Husson College	Bangor, ME
Braves	Ottawa University	Ottawa, KS
Braves	Pembroke State University	Pembroke, NC
Braves	West Georgia, State University of	Carrollton, GA
Brewers	Vassar College	Poughkeepsie, NY
Bridges, The	Brooklyn College of CUNY	Brooklyn, NY
Britons	Albion College	Albion, MI
Bronchos	Central Oklahoma, University of	Edmond, OK
Broncos	Boise State University	Boise, ID
Broncos	Cal State Poly University–Pomona	Pomona, CA
Broncos	Fayetteville State University	Fayetteville, NC
Broncos	Hastings College	Hastings, NE
Broncos	Santa Clara University	Santa Clara, CA
Broncos	Western Michigan University	Kalamazoo, MI
Broncs	Rider University	Lawrenceville, NJ
Broncs	Texas–Pan American, University of	Edinburg, TX
Bruins	Bellevue University	Bellevue, NE
Bruins	Belmont University	Nashville, TN
Bruins	Bethany College	Scotts Valley, CA
Bruins	Cal–Los Angeles, University of (UCLA)	Los Angeles, CA
Bruins	George Fox University	Newberg, OR
Buccaneers	Barry University	Miami, FL
Buccaneers	Beloit College	Beloit, WI
Buccaneers	Charleston Southern University	Charleston, SC
Buccaneers	Christian Brothers University	Memphis, TN
Buccaneers	East Tennessee State University	Johnson City, TN
Buccaneers	Massachusetts Maritime Academy	Buzzards Bay, MA
Buccaneers	Virgin Islands, University of the	St. Thomas, VI
Buckeyes	Ohio State University	Columbus, OH

Senior Colleges and Universities—United States
Alphabetic Listing by Nickname/Mascot

Nickname/Mascot	Institution Name	Location
Buffaloes	Arkansas Baptist College	Little Rock, AR
Buffaloes	Colorado, University of	Boulder, CO
Buffaloes	Milligan College	Milligan College, TN
Buffaloes	West Texas A&M University	Canyon, TX
Builders	Newport News Apprentice Institute	Newport News, VA
Bulldogs	Adrian College	Adrian, MI
Bulldogs	Alabama A & M University	Normal, AL
Bulldogs	Barat College	Lake Forest, IL
Bulldogs	Barton College	Wilson, NC
Bulldogs	Bowie State University	Bowie, MD
Bulldogs	Bryant College	Smithfield, RI
Bulldogs	Butler University	Indianapolis, IN
Bulldogs	Citadel, The	Charleston, SC
Bulldogs	Cal State University—Fresno State	Fresno, CA
Bulldogs	Concordia University of Nebraska	Seward, NE
Bulldogs	Cumberland University	Lebanon, TN
Bulldogs	DeSales University	Center Valley, PA
Bulldogs	Drake University	Des Moines, IA
Bulldogs	Ferris State University	Big Rapids, MI
Bulldogs	Fisk University	Nashville, TN
Bulldogs	Gardner-Webb University	Boiling Springs, NC
Bulldogs	Georgia, University of	Athens, GA
Bulldogs	Gonzaga University	Spokane, WA
Bulldogs	Jarvis Christian College	Hawkins, TX
Bulldogs	Knoxville College	Knoxville, TN
Bulldogs	Louisiana Technical University	Ruston, LA
Bulldogs	McPherson College	McPherson, KS
Bulldogs	Minnesota—Duluth, University of	Duluth, MN
Bulldogs	Mississippi State University	Starkville, MS
Bulldogs	Montana Western, University of	Dillon, MT
Bulldogs	North Carolina—Asheville, University of	Asheville, NC
Bulldogs	Redlands, University of the	Redlands, CA
Bulldogs	Samford University	Birmingham, AL
Bulldogs	Selma University	Selma, AL
Bulldogs	South Carolina State College	Orangeburg, SC
Bulldogs	Southwestern Oklahoma State University	Weatherford, OK
Bulldogs	Tennessee Wesleyan College	Athens, TN
Bulldogs	Texas Lutheran University	Seguin, TX
Bulldogs	Tougaloo College	Tougaloo, MS
Bulldogs	Truman State University	Kirksville, MO
Bulldogs	Union College	Barbourville, KY

Senior Colleges and Universities—United States
Alphabetic Listing by Nickname/Mascot

Nickname/Mascot	Institution Name	Location
Bulldogs	Union University	Jackson, TN
Bulldogs	Wilberforce University	Wilberforce, OH
Bulldogs	Wingate University	Wingate, NC
Bulldogs	Yale University	New Haven, CT
Bullets	Gettysburg College	Gettysburg, PA
Bulls	South Florida, University of	Tampa, FL
Bulls	SUNY—Buffalo	Buffalo, NY

C

Nickname/Mascot	Institution Name	Location
Cadets	Norwich University	Northfield, VT
Cadets or Black Knights	U.S. Military Academy	West Point, NY
Camels	Campbell University	Buies Creek, NC
Camels	Connecticut College	New London, CT
Cannoneers	Pratt Institute	Brooklyn, NY
Captains	Christopher Newport University	Newport News, VA
Cardinal, The	Stanford University	Palo Alto, CA
Cardinals	Andrews University	Berrien Springs, MI
Cardinals	Ball State University	Muncie, IN
Cardinals	Catholic University of America	Washington, DC
Cardinals	Concordia University	Ann Arbor, MI
Cardinals	Crichton College	Memphis, TN
Cardinals	Lamar University	Beaumont, TX
Cardinals	Louisville, University of	Louisville, KY
Cardinals	Massachusetts College of Pharmacy & Health	Boston, MA
Cardinals	North Central College	Naperville, IL
Cardinals	Otterbein College	Westerville, OH
Cardinals	Saginaw Valley State University	University Center, MI
Cardinals	St. John Fisher College	Rochester, NY
Cardinals	St. Mary's University of Minnesota	Winona, MN
Cardinals	SUNY—Plattsburgh	Plattsburgh, NY
Cardinals	Wesleyan University	Middletown, CT
Cardinals	Wheeling Jesuit University	Wheeling, WV
Cardinals	William Jewell College	Liberty, MO
Cardinals	York College of CUNY	Jamaica, NY
Catamounts	Vermont, University of	Burlington, VT
Catamounts	Western Carolina University	Cullowhee, NC
Cavaliers	Aquinas College	Nashville, TN
Cavaliers	Cabrini College	Radnor, PA
Cavaliers	Concordia University	Portland, OR
Cavaliers	East Coast Bible College	Charlotte, NC

Senior Colleges and Universities—United States

Alphabetic Listing by Nickname/Mascot

Nickname/Mascot	Institution Name	Location
Cavaliers	Montreat College	Montreat, NC
Cavaliers	St. Gregory's University	Shawnee, OK
Cavaliers	Virginia, University of	Charlottesville, VA
Cavaliers	Walsh University	Canton, OH
Celtics	Carlow College (Women)	Pittsburgh, PA
Celts	St. Thomas, University of	Houston, TX
Centaurs	Purdue University—North Central	Westville, IN
Chanticleers	Coastal Carolina University	Conway, SC
Chaparrals	Lubbock Christian University	Lubbock, TX
Chargers	Alabama—Huntsville, University of	Huntsville, AL
Chargers	Atlanta Christian College	East Point, GA
Chargers	Briar Cliff University	Sioux City, IA
Chargers	Capitol College	Laurel, MD
Chargers	Colby-Sawyer College	New London, NH
Chargers	Cypress College	Cypress, CA
Chargers	Dominican College	Orangeburg, NY
Chargers	Hillsdale College	Hillsdale, MI
Chargers	Lancaster Bible College	Lancaster, PA
Chargers	New Haven, University of	West Haven, CT
Chargers	Southeastern Baptist College	Laurel, MS
Chieftans	Stonehill College	North Easton, MA
Chippewas	Central Michigan University	Mt. Pleasant, MI
Choctaws	Mississippi College	Clinton, MS
Clippers	Concordia College	Bronxville, NY
Clippers	Maine—Machias, University of	Machias, ME
Clippers	Webb Institute	Glen Cove, LI, NY
Cobbers	Concordia College	Moorhead, MN
Cobras	Coker College	Hartsville, SC
Cobras	Virginia Intermont College	Bristol, VA
Colonels	Centre College	Danville, KY
Colonels	Curry College	Milton, MA
Colonels	Eastern Kentucky University	Richmond, KY
Colonels	Nicholls State University	Thibodaux, LA
Colonels	Wilkes University	Wilkes-Barre, PA
Colonials	George Washington University	Washington, DC
Colonials	Georgia College and State University	Milledgeville, GA
Colonials	Long Island University—Southhampton	Southhampton, NY
Colonials	Robert Morris College	Coraopolis, PA
Colonials	Western Connecticut State University	Danbury, CT
Comets	Mayville State University	Mayville, ND
Comets	Olivet College	Olivet, MI
Comets	Pillsbury Baptist Bible College	Owatonna, MN

Senior Colleges and Universities—United States
Alphabetic Listing by Nickname/Mascot

Nickname/Mascot	Institution Name	Location
Comets	Texas–Dallas, University of	Richardson, TX
Commodores	Vanderbilt University	Nashville, TN
Conquerors	Midwest Christian College	Oklahoma City, OK
Conquerors	Piedmont Baptist College	Winston-Salem, NC
Continentals	Hamilton College	Clinton, NY
Cornhuskers	Nebraska, University of	Lincoln, NE
Corsairs	Massachusetts–Dartmouth, University of	North Dartmouth, MA
Cossacks	Sonoma State University	Rohnert Park, CA
Cougars	Averett College	Danville, VA
Cougars	Azusa Pacific College	Azusa, CA
Cougars	Brigham Young University	Provo, UT
Cougars	Cal State University–San Marcos	San Marcos, CA
Cougars	Caldwell College	Caldwell, NJ
Cougars	Carver Bible College	Atlanta, GA
Cougars	Charleston, College of	Charleston, SC
Cougars	Chatham College (Women)	Pittsburgh, PA
Cougars	Clark University	Worcester, MA
Cougars	Clearwater Christian College	Clearwater, FL
Cougars	Colorado Christian University	Lakewood, CO
Cougars	Columbia College	Columbia, MO
Cougars	Columbus State University	Columbus, GA
Cougars	Concordia University	River Forest, IL
Cougars	Chicago State University	Chicago, IL
Cougars	Houston, University of	Houston, TX
Cougars	Kean University	Union, NJ
Cougars	Medgar Evers College of CUNY	Brooklyn, NY
Cougars	Mid-Continent College	Mayfield, KY
Cougars	Minnesota–Morris, University of	Morris, MN
Cougars	Misericordia, College	Dallas, PA
Cougars	Mt. Vernon Nazarene College	Mt. Vernon, OH
Cougars	Mountain State University	Beckley, WV
Cougars	Southern Illinois University–Edwardsville	Edwardsville, IL
Cougars	Sioux Falls, University of	Sioux Falls, SD
Cougars	Spring Arbor University	Spring Arbor, MI
Cougars	St. Francis, University of	Ft. Wayne, IN
Cougars	St. Xavier University	Chicago, IL
Cougars	Vennard College	University Park, IA
Cougars	Washington Bible College	Lanham, MD
Cougars	Washington State University	Pullman, WA
Cowboys	Hardin-Simmons University	Abilene, TX
Cowboys	McNeese State University	Lake Charles, LA

Senior Colleges and Universities—United States

Alphabetic Listing by Nickname/Mascot

Nickname/Mascot	Institution Name	Location
Cowboys	New Mexico Highlands University	Las Vegas, NM
Cowboys	Oklahoma State University	Stillwater, OK
Cowboys	Wyoming, University of	Laramie, WY
Coyotes	Albertson College of Idaho	Caldwell, ID
Coyotes	Cal State University—San Bernadino	San Bernadino, CA
Coyotes	Kansas Wesleyan University	Salina, KS
Coyotes	South Dakota, University of	Vermillion, SD
Crimson	Harvard University	Cambridge, MA
Crimson Eagles	Philadelphia Biblical University	Langhorne, PA
Crimson Storm	Southern Nazarene University	Bethany, OK
Crimson Tide	Alabama, University of	Tuscaloosa, AL
Crimson Wave	Calumet College of St. Joseph	Whiting, IN
Crusaders	Alvernia College	Reading, PA
Crusaders	Belmont Abbey College	Belmont, NC
Crusaders	Capital University	Columbus, OH
Crusaders	Cardinal Stritch University	Milwaukee, WI
Crusaders	Christendom College	Winchester, VA
Crusaders	Circleville Bible College	Circleville, OH
Crusaders	Clarke College	Dubuque, IA
Crusaders	Dallas Christian College	Dallas, TX
Crusaders	Dallas, University of	Irving, TX
Crusaders	Eastern Nazarene College	Quincy, MA
Crusaders	Evangel University	Springfield, MO
Crusaders	Great Lakes Christian College	Lansing, MI
Crusaders	Holy Cross, College of the	Worcester, MA
Crusaders	Incarnate Word, University of the	San Antonio, TX
Crusaders	John Wesley College	High Point, NC
Crusaders	Madonna University	Livonia, MI
Crusaders	Manhattan Christian College	Manhattan, KS
Crusaders	Maranatha Baptist Bible College	Watertown, WI
Crusaders	Mary Hardin—Baylor, University of	Belton, TX
Crusaders	Mt. Mary College (Women)	Manitowoc, WI
Crusaders	North Greenville College	Tigerville, SC
Crusaders	Northwest Christian College	Eugene, OR
Crusaders	Northwest Nazarene College	Nampa, ID
Crusaders	Point Loma Nazarene University	San Diego, CA
Crusaders	Southeastern College	Lakeland, FL
Crusaders	Susquehanna University	Selinsgrove, PA
Crusaders	Tennessee Temple University	Chattanooga, TN
Crusaders	Valparaiso University	Valparaiso, IN
Crusaders	Villa Maria College	Erie, PA

Senior Colleges and Universities—United States
Alphabetic Listing by Nickname/Mascot

Nickname/Mascot	Institution Name	Location
Crusaders	William Carey College	Hattiesburg, MS
Cyclones	Centenary College	Hackettstown, NJ
Cyclones	Mills College (Women)	Oakland, CA
Cyclones	Iowa State University	Ames, IA

D

Deacons	Bloomfield College	Bloomfield, NJ
Deacons	Eugene Bible College	Eugene, OR
Defenders	Baptist Bible College	Clarks Summit, PA
Defenders	Dordt College	Sioux Center, IA
Delta Devils	Mississippi Valley State University	Itta Bena, MS
Demon Deacons	Wake Forest University	Winston-Salem, NC
Demons	Northwestern State University	Natchitoches, LA
Devils	Fairleigh-Dickinson University—Florham	Madison, NJ
Devils	Sciences in Philadelphia, University of the	Philadelphia, PA
Diplomats	Franklin & Marshall College	Lancaster, PA
Dolphins	Jacksonville University	Jacksonville, FL
Dolphins	Le Moyne College	Syracuse, NY
Dolphins	Mt. St. Vincent, College of	Riverdale, NY
Dolphins	Staten Island of CUNY, College of	Staten Island, NY
Dons	San Francisco, University of	San Francisco, CA
Dragons	Drexel University	Philadelphia, PA
Dragons	Lane College	Jackson, TN
Dragons	Minnesota State University Moorhead	Moorhead, MN
Dragons	Tiffin University	Tiffin, OH
Drovers	Science & Arts of Oklahoma, University of	Chickasha, OK
Ducks	Oregon, University of	Eugene, OR
Ducks	Stevens Institute of Technology	Hoboken, NJ
DuHawks	Loras College	Dubuque, IA
Dukes	Duquesne University	Pittsburgh, PA
Dukes	James Madison University	Harrisonburg, VA
Dukes	Penn State University—DuBois	DuBois, PA
Dust Devils	Texas A&M International University	Laredo, TX
Dutch	Central College	Pella, IA
Dutchmen	Union College	Schenectady, NY

E

Eagles	Alice Lloyd College	Pippa Passes, KY
Eagles	American University	Washington, DC
Eagles	Asbury College	Wilmore, KY

Alphabetic Listing by Nickname/Mascot

Nickname/Mascot	Institution Name	Location
Eagles	Ashland University	Ashland, OH
Eagles	Avila College	Kansas City, MO
Eagles	Bartlesville Wesleyan College	Bartlesville, OK
Eagles	Bay Ridge Christian College	Kendleton, TX
Eagles	Benedictine University	Lisle, IL
Eagles	Biola University	La Mirada, CA
Eagles	Boston College	Chestnut Hill, MA
Eagles	Bridgewater College	Bridgewater, VA
Eagles	Carson-Newman College	Jefferson City, TN
Eagles	Central Methodist College	Fayette, MO
Eagles	Chadron State College	Chadron, NE
Eagles	Concordia University of California	Irvine, CA
Eagles	Coppin State College	Baltimore, MD
Eagles	Dallas Bible College	Dallas, TX
Eagles	Daniel Webster College	Nashua, NH
Eagles	Eastern University	St. Davids, PA
Eagles	Eastern Michigan University	Ypsilanti, MI
Eagles	Eastern Washington University	Cheney, WA
Eagles	Edgewood College	Madison, WI
Eagles	Embry-Riddle Aeronautical University	Daytona Beach, FL
Eagles	Embry-Riddle Aeronautical University	Prescott, AZ
Eagles	Emmaus Bible College	Dubuque, IA
Eagles	Emory University	Atlanta, GA
Eagles	Faith Baptist Bible College	Ankeny, IA
Eagles	Faulkner University	Montgomery, AL
Eagles	Florida Gulf Coast University	Ft. Myers, FL
Eagles	Georgia Southern University	Statesboro, GA
Eagles	Green Mountain College	Poultney, VT
Eagles	Jimmy Swaggart Bible College	Baton Rouge, LA
Eagles	Judson College	Elgin, IL
Eagles	Juniata College	Huntingdon, PA
Eagles	Lambuth University	Jackson, TN
Eagles	Mary Washington College	Fredericksburg, VA
Eagles	Maryland Bible College & Seminary	Baltimore, MD
Eagles	Messenger College	Joplin, MO
Eagles	Midway College (Women)	Midway, KY
Eagles	Morehead State University	Morehead, KY
Eagles	National-Louis University	Chicago, IL
Eagles	North Carolina Central University	Durham, NC
Eagles	Northwest College	Kirkland, WA
Eagles	Northwestern College	St. Paul, MN
Eagles	Oklahoma Christian University	Oklahoma City, OK

Senior Colleges and Universities—United States
Alphabetic Listing by Nickname/Mascot

Nickname/Mascot	Institution Name	Location
Eagles	Oklahoma Wesleyan University	Bartlesville, OK
Eagles	Ozarks, University of the	Clarksville, AR
Eagles	Pacific Coast Baptist Bible College	San Dimas, CA
Eagles	Pensacola Christian College	Pensacola, FL
Eagles	Reinhardt College	Waleska, GA
Eagles	Rhema Bible College	Broken Arrow, OK
Eagles	Robert Morris College–Springfield	Springfield, IL
Eagles	Southern Baptist College	Walnut Ridge, AR
Eagles	Southwestern Christian University	Bethany, OK
Eagles	Southwestern College	Phoenix, AZ
Eagles	St. Elizabeth (Women), College of	Morristown, NJ
Eagles	St. Mary's College of Ave Maria University	Orchard Lake, MI
Eagles	Sierra Nevada College	Incline Village,NV
Eagles	Teikyo Post University	Waterbury, CT
Eagles	Toccoa Falls College	Toccoa Falls, GA
Eagles	Trinity Baptist College	Jacksonville, FL
Eagles	Williams Baptist College	Walnut Ridge, AR
Eagles	Winthrop University	Rock Hill, SC
Eagles	Wisconsin—LaCrosse, University of	LaCrosse, WI
Engineers	Massachusetts Institute of Technology (MIT)	Cambridge, MA
Engineers or Red Hawks	Rensselaer Polytechnic Institute (RPI)	Troy, NY
Engineers	Rose-Hulman Institute of Technology	Terre Haute, IN
Engineers	Worcester Polytechnic Institute	Worcester, MA
Ephmen/Ephwomen	Williams College	Williamstown, MA
Eutectics	St. Louis College of Pharmacy	St. Louis, MO.
Evangels	Mid-America Bible College	Oklahoma City, OK
Explorers	La Salle University	Philadelphia, PA
Express, The	Wells College (Women)	Aurora, NY

F

Nickname/Mascot	Institution Name	Location
Falcons	Albertus Magnus College	New Haven, CT
Falcons	Bentley College	Waltham, MA
Falcons	Bowling Green State University	Bowling Green, OH
Falcons	Cedar Crest College (Women)	Allentown, PA
Falcons	Concordia University Wisconsin	Mequon, WI
Falcons	Detroit College of Business	Dearborn, MI
Falcons	Fairmont State College	Fairmont, WV
Falcons	Fisher College	Boston, MA
Falcons	Fitchburg State College	Fitchburg, MA
Falcons	Friends University	Wichita, KS

Senior Colleges and Universities—United St.s
Alphabetic Listing by Nickname/Mascot

Nickname/Mascot	Institution Name	Location
Falcons	Kansas City College & Bible School	Overland Park, KS
Falcons	Messiah College	Grantham, PA
Falcons	Montevallo, University of	Montevallo, AL
Falcons	Parks College of St. Louis University	Cahokia, IL
Falcons	Pfeiffer University	Misenheimer, NC
Falcons	St. Augustine's College	Raleigh, NC
Falcons	Seattle Pacific University	Seattle, WA
Falcons	Taylor University–Ft. Wayne	Ft. Wayne, IN
Falcons	Texas–Permian Basin, University of	Odessa, TX
Falcons	U.S. Air Force Academy	Colorado Springs, CO
Falcons	Wisconsin–River Falls, University of	River Falls, WI
Fightin' Blue Hens	Delaware, University of	Newark, DE
Fightin' Indians	Haskell Indian Nations University	Lawrence, KS
Fighting Bees/Queen Bees	St. Ambrose University	Davenport, IA
Fighting Illini	Illinois, University of	Urbana/ Champagne, IL
Fighting Irish	Notre Dame University	South Bend, IN
Fighting Koalas	Columbia College (Women)	Columbia, SC
Fighting Muskies	Muskingum College	New Concord, OH
Fighting Saints	Carroll College	Helena, MT
Fighting Saints	Mt. Senario College	Ladysmith, WI
Fighting Saints	St. Francis, University of	Joliet, IL
Fighting Saints	St. Joseph in Vermont, College of	Rutland, VT
Fighting Scots	Edinboro University of Pennsylvania	Edinboro, PA
Fighting Scots	Gordon College	Wenham, MA
Fighting Scots	Maryville College	Maryville, TN
Fighting Scots	Monmouth College	Monmouth, IL
Fighting Scots	Ohio Valley College	Parkersburg, WV
Fighting Scots	Wooster, College of	Wooster, OH
Fighting Sioux	North Dakota, University of	Grand Forks, ND
Firebirds	District of Columbia, University of the	Washington, DC
Flames	Atlantic Union College	S. Lancaster, MA
Flames	Free Will Baptist Bible College	Nashville, TN
Flames	Illinois–Chicago, University of	Chicago, IL
Flames	Lee University	Cleveland, TN
Flames	Liberty University	Lynchburg, VA
Flames	Roanoke Bible College	Elizabeth City, NC
Flames	St. Mary (Women), College of	Omaha, NE
Flyers	Dayton, University of	Dayton, OH
Flyers	Lewis University	Romeoville, IL

Senior Colleges and Universities—United States
Alphabetic Listing by Nickname/Mascot

Nickname/Mascot	Institution Name	Location
Flyers	Maharishi University of Management	Fairfield, IA
Flyers	Mercy College	Dobbs Ferry, NY
Flying Dutch	Hope College	Hope, MI
Flying Dutchmen	Lebanon Valley College	Annville, PA
Flying Fleet/Lady Fleet	Erskine College	Due West, SC
Fords	Haverford College	Haverford, PA
Foresters	Huntington College	Huntington, IN
Foresters	Lake Forest College	Lake Forest, IL
Friars	Providence College	Providence, RI
Fundamentalists	Fairhaven Baptist College	Chesterton, IN

G

Nickname/Mascot	Institution Name	Location
Gaels	Iona College	New Rochelle, NY
Gaels	St. Mary's College of California	Moraga, CA
Gamecocks	Jacksonville State University	Jacksonville, AL
Gamecocks	South Carolina, University of	Columbia, SC
Garnet Tide	Swarthmore College	Swarthmore, PA
Gators	Allegheny College	Meadville, PA
Gators	Pine Manor College (Women)	Chestnut Hill, MA
Gators	Florida, University of	Gainesville, FL
Gators	Notre Dame of MD (Women), College of	Baltimore, MD
Gators	Russell Sage College (Women)	Troy, NY
Gators	San Francisco State University	San Francisco, CA
Gauchos	Cal–Santa Barbara, University of	Santa Barbara, CA
Generals	Eisenhower College	Seneca Falls, NY
Generals	Washington & Lee University	Lexington, VA
Gents/Ladies	Centenary College of Louisiana	Shreveport, LA
Geoducks	Evergreen State College	Olympia, WA
Giants	Keystone College	La Plume, PA
Gold Rush/Nuggets	Xavier University of Louisiana	New Orleans, LA
Golden Bears	Cal–Berkeley, University of	Berkeley, CA
Golden Bears	Concordia University	St. Paul, MN
Golden Bears	Kutztown University	Kutztown, PA
Golden Bears	Miles College	Birmingham, AL
Golden Bears	Morgan State University	Baltimore, MD
Golden Bears	Western New England College	Springfield, MA
Golden Bears	West Virginia University Institute of Technology	Montgomery, WV
Golden Bulls	Johnson C. Smith University	Charlotte, NC
Golden Eagles	Cal State University–Los Angeles	Los Angeles, CA
Golden Eagles	Charleston, University of	Charleston, WV

Senior Colleges and Universities—United States

Alphabetic Listing by Nickname/Mascot

Nickname/Mascot	Institution Name	Location
Golden Eagles	Cincinnati Bible College & Seminary	Cincinnati, OH
Golden Eagles	Clarion University	Clarion, PA
Golden Eagles	Cornerstone University	Grand Rapids, MI
Golden Eagles	John Brown University	Siloam Springs, AR
Golden Eagles	La Sierra University	Riverside, CA
Golden Eagles	Marquette University	Milwaukee, WI
Golden Eagles	Minnesota—Crookston, University of	Crookston, MN
Golden Eagles	Northeastern Illinois University	Chicago, IL
Golden Eagles	Oral Roberts University	Tulsa, OK
Golden Eagles	Southern Idaho, College of	Twin Falls, ID
Golden Eagles	Southern Mississippi, University of	Hattiesburg, MS
Golden Eagles	St. Joseph's College—Suffolk	Patchogue, LI, NY
Golden Eagles	SUNY—Brockport	Brockport, NY
Golden Eagles	Tennessee Technical University	Cookeville, TN
Golden Falcons	Felician College	Lodi, NJ
Golden Flashes	Kent State University	Kent, OH
Golden Flyers	Nazareth College	Rochester, NY
Golden Gophers	Minnesota, University of	Minneapolis, MN
Golden Griffins	Canisius College	Buffalo, NY
Golden Griffins	Golden Gate University	San Francisco, CA
Golden Grizzlies	Oakland University	Rochester, MI
Golden Gusties	Gustavus Adolphus College	St. Peter, MN
Golden Hawks	Mercer College	Atlanta, GA
Golden Hurricanes	Tulsa, University of	Tulsa, OK
Golden Knights	Central Florida, University of	Orlando, FL
Golden Knights	Clarkson University	Potsdam, NY
Golden Knights	Gannon University	Erie, PA
Golden Knights	St. Rose, College of	Albany, NY
Golden Lions	Arkansas—Pine Bluff, University of	Pine Bluff, AR
Golden Lions	Dowling College	Oakdale, NY
Golden Panthers	Florida International University	Miami, FL
Golden Rams	Albany State University	Albany, GA
Golden Rams	West Chester University of Pennsylvania	West Chester, PA
Golden Tigers	Brenau University (Women)	Gainesville, GA
Golden Tigers	Tuskegee University	Tuskegee, AL
Golden Tornadoes	Geneva College	Beaver Falls, PA
Gophers	Goucher College	Baltimore, MD
Gorillas	Pittsburg State University	Pittsburg, KS
Gorloks	Webster University	Webster Groves, MO
Gothic Knights	New Jersey City University	Jersey City, NJ
Governors	Austin Peay State University	Clarksville, TN

Senior Colleges and Universities—United States
Alphabetic Listing by Nickname/Mascot

Nickname/Mascot	Institution Name	Location
Great Danes	SUNY–Albany	Albany, NY
Green & Gold	Hollins University (Women)	Roanoke, VA
Green Knights	St. Norbert College	De Pere, WI
Green Knights	Vermont Technical College	Randolph Center, VT
Green Terrors	McDaniel College	Westminster, MD
Green Wave	Newcomb College	New Orleans, LA
Green Wave	Tulane University	New Orleans, LA
Grenadiers	Indiana University–Southeast	New Albany, IN
Greyhounds	Assumption College	Worcester, MA
Greyhounds	Eastern New Mexico University	Portales, NM
Greyhounds	Indianapolis, University of	Indianapolis, IN
Greyhounds	Loyola College	Baltimore, MD
Greyhounds	Moravian College	Bethlehem, PA
Griffins	Chestnut Hill College	Philadelphia, PA
Griffins	Fontbonne College	St. Louis, MO
Griffins	Gwynedd Mercy College	Gwynedd Valley, PA
Griffins	Westminster College	Salt Lake City, UT
Griffons	Missouri Western State College	St. Joseph, MO
Grizzlies	Adams State College	Alamosa, CO
Grizzlies	Franklin College	Franklin, IN
Grizzlies	Montana, University of	Missoula, MT
Gryphons	Sarah Lawrence College	Bronxville, NY

H

Nickname/Mascot	Institution Name	Location
Hardrockers	South Dakota School of Mines & Technology	Rapid City, SD
Hatters	Stetson University	Deland, FL
Hawkeyes	Iowa, University of	Iowa City, IA
Hawks	Becker College	Worcester, MA
Hawks	Christian Heritage College	El Cajon, CA
Hawks	Hartford University + Hartford College for Women	West Hartford, CT
Hawks	Hartwick College	Oneonta, NY
Hawks	Hilbert College	Hamburg, NY
Hawks	Holy Names College	Oakland, CA
Hawks	Hunter College of CUNY	New York, NY
Hawks	Huntingdon College	Montgomery, AL
Hawks	Maryland–Eastern Shore, University of	Princess Anne, MD
Hawks	Monmouth University	W. Long Branch, NJ
Hawks	Quincy University	Quincy, IL

Senior Colleges and Universities—United States
Alphabetic Listing by Nickname/Mascot

Nickname/Mascot	Institution Name	Location
Hawks	Rockhurst College	Kansas City, MO
Hawks	Roger Williams University	Bristol, RI
Hawks	Shorter College	Rome, GA
Hawks	Southeastern University	Washington, DC
Hawks	St. Anselm College	Manchester, NH
Hawks	St. Joseph's University	Philadelphia, PA
Hawks	SUNY—New Paltz	New Paltz, NY
Heralds	Central Christian Bible College	Moberly, MO
Herons	William Smith College	Geneva, NY
Highland Cavaliers	Virginia—Wise, University of	Wise, VA
Highlanders	Cal—Riverside, University of	Riverside, CA
Highlanders	Houghton College	Houghton, NY
Highlanders	Mac Murray College	Jacksonville, IL
Highlanders	New Jersey Institute of Technology	Newark, NJ
Highlanders	Radford University	Radford, VA
Hilltoppers	St. Edward's University	Austin, TX
Hilltoppers	West Liberty State College	West Liberty, WV
Hilltoppers	Western Kentucky University	Bowling Green, KY
Hokies or Gobblers	Virginia Polytechnic Institute and State University (Virginia Tech)	Blacksburg, VA
Hoosiers	Indiana University	Bloomington, IN
Horned Frogs	Texas Christian University (TCU)	Ft. Worth, TX
Hornets	Alabama State University	Montgomery, AL
Hornets	Cal State University—Sacramento	Sacramento, CA
Hornets	Concordia College	Selma, AL
Hornets	Delaware State University	Dover, DE
Hornets	Emporia State University	Emporia, KS
Hornets	Harris-Stowe State College	St. Louis, MO
Hornets	Kalamazoo College	Kalamazoo, MI
Hornets	Lynchburg College	Lynchburg, VA
Hornets	Lyndon State College	Lyndonville, VT
Hornets	Morris College	Sumter, SC
Hornets	Shenandoah University	Winchester, VA
Hornets	Southern Poly State University	Marietta, GA
Hoyas	De Vry Institute of Technology	Atlanta, GA
Hoyas	Georgetown University	Washington, DC
Hurricanes	Georgia Southwestern State University	Americus, GA
Hurricanes	Miami, University of	Miami, FL
Huskies	Bloomsburg University of Pennsylvania	Bloomsburg, PA
Huskies	Connecticut, University of	Storrs, CT
Huskies	Houston Baptist University	Houston, TX
Huskies	Michigan Technical University	Houghton, MI

Senior Colleges and Universities—United States
Alphabetic Listing by Nickname/Mascot

Nickname/Mascot	Institution Name	Location
Huskies	Northeastern University	Boston, MA
Huskies	Northern Illinois University	DeKalb, IL
Huskies	Southern Maine, University of	Gorham, ME
Huskies	St. Cloud State University	St. Cloud, MN
Huskies	Washington, University of	Seattle, WA
Hustlin' Owls	Oregon Institute of Technology	Klamath Falls, OR

I

Ichabods/Lady Blues	Washburn University	Topeka, KS
Indians	Arkansas State University	Jonesboro, AR
Indians	Catawba College	Salisbury, NC
Indians	Indiana University of Pennsylvania	Indiana, PA
Indians	Louisiana–Monroe, University of	Monroe, LA
Indians	McMurry University	Abilene, TX
Indians	Midwestern State University	Wichita Falls, TX
Indians	Newberry College	Newberry, SC
Indians or Utahkians	Southeast Missouri State University	Cape Giradeau, MO
Inferno	Alverno College (Women)	Milwaukee, WI
Islanders	Texas A & M University–Corpus Christi	Corpus Christi, TX

J

Jackrabbits	South Dakota State University	Brookings, SD
Jaguars	Augusta State University	Augusta, GA
Jaguars	Indiana U.–Purdue University–Indianapolis	Indianapolis, IN
Jaguars	South Alabama, University of	Mobile, AL
Jaguars	Southern University and A&M College	Baton Rouge, LA
Jaguars	Spelman College (Women)	Atlanta, GA
Jaspers	Manhattan College	Bronx, NY
Javelinas	Texas A & M University–Kingsville	Kingsville, TX
Jayhawks	Kansas, University of	Lawrence, KS
Jets	Newman University	Wichita, KS
Jimmies	Jamestown College	Jamestown, ND
Johnnies	St. John's University	Collegeville, MN
Judges	Brandeis University	Waltham, MA
Jumbos	Tufts University	Medford, MA

K

Kangaroos	Austin College	Sherman, TX
Kangaroos	Missouri–Kansas City, University of	Kansas City, MO

Senior Colleges and Universities—United States

Alphabetic Listing by Nickname/Mascot

Nickname/Mascot	Institution Name	Location
Keelhaulers	California Maritime Academy	Vallejo, CA
Keydets	Virginia Military Institute (VMI)	Lexington, VA
King's Men	Concordia Theological Seminary	Ft. Wayne, IN
Kingsmen/Regals	California Lutheran University	Thousand Oaks, CA
Knights	Bellarmine College	Louisville, KY
Knights	Calvin College	Grand Rapids, MI
Knights	Carleton College	Northfield, MN
Knights	Fairleigh-Dickinson University—Teaneck	Teaneck, NJ
Knights	Immanuel Lutheran College	Eau Claire, WI
Knights	Indiana University—Kokomo	Kokomo, IN
Knights	Kentucky Christian College	Grayson, KY
Knights	Lynn University	Boca Raton, FL
Knights	Marian College	Indianapolis, IN
Knights	Martin Luther College	New Ulm, MN
Knights	Mt. St. Mary College	Newburgh, NY
Knights	Neumann College	Aston, PA
Knights	Northwood University	Cedar Hill, TX
Knights	Nova Southeastern University	Davie, FL
Knights	Queens College of CUNY	Flushing, NY
Knights	Sante Fe, College of	Santa Fe, NM
Knights	Simpson College	San Francisco, CA
Knights	Southern University at New Orleans	New Orleans, LA
Knights	Southern Virginia University	Buena Vista, VA
Knights	Southwestern Adventist University	Keene, TX
Knights	St. Andrew's Presbyterian College	Laurinburg, NC
Knights	SUNY—Geneseo	Geneseo, NY
Knights	Warner Pacific College	Portland, OR
Knights	Wartburg College	Waverly, IA
Kohawks	Coe College	Cedar Rapids, IA

L

Lady Eagles	Judson College for Women	Marion, AL
Lakers	Clayton College and State University	Morrow, GA
Lakers	Grand Valley State University	Allendale, MI
Lakers	Lake Superior State University	Sault Ste. Marie, MI
Lakers	Lakewood College	Lakewood, OH
Lakers	Mercyhurst College	Erie, PA
Lakers	Silver Lake College	Manitowoc, WI
Lakers	SUNY—Oswego	Oswego, NY
Lakers	Purdue University—Calumet	Hammond, IN
Lakers	Roosevelt University	Chicago, IL

Senior Colleges and Universities—United States
Alphabetic Listing by Nickname/Mascot

Nickname/Mascot	Institution Name	Location
Lancers	California Baptist University	Riverside, CA
Lancers	Detroit Bible College	Farmington Hills, MI
Lancers	Grace College & Seminary	Winona Lake, IN
Lancers	Longwood College	Farmville, VA
Lancers	Mt. Marty College	Yankton, SD
Lancers	William Tyndale College	Farmington Hills,MI
Lancers	Worcester State College	Worcester, MA
Lasers	Lasell College	Newton, MA
Leathernecks/Westerwinds	Western Illinois University	Macomb, IL
Leopards	La Verne, University of	La Verne, CA
Leopards	Lafayette College	Easton, PA
Leopards	Wentworth Institute of Technology	Boston, MA
Lightning	Goldey-Beacom College	Wilmington, DE
Lightning	Lehman College of CUNY	Bronx, NY
Lions	Albright College	Reading, PA
Lions	Bryan College	Dayton, TN
Lions	Barnard College (Women)	New York, NY
Lions	Columbia University	New York, NY
Lions	East Texas State University	Commerce, TX
Lions	Emmanuol Collogo	Franklin Springs, GA
Lions	Emerson—Massachusetts College of Art	Boston, MA
Lions	Finlandia University	Hancock, MI
Lions	Florida Memorial College	Opa Locka, FL
Lions	Freed-Hardeman University	Henderson, TN
Lions	Georgian Court College (Women)	Lakewood, NJ
Lions	Langston University	Langston, OK
Lions	Latin American Bible Institute	LaPuente, CA
Lions	Lincoln University	Philadelphia, PA
Lions	Loyola Marymount University	Los Angeles, CA
Lions	Mars Hill College	Mars Hill, NC
Lions	Missouri Southern State College	Joplin, MO
Lions	Molloy College	Rockville Center, NY
Lions	Mt. St. Joseph, College of	Cincinnati, OH
Lions	New Jersey, College of	Ewing, NJ
Lions	North Alabama, University of	Florence, AL
Lions	Paine College	Augusta, GA
Lions	Patten College	Oakland, CA
Lions	Penn State University—Abington	Abington, PA
Lions	Penn State University—McKeesport	McKeesport, PA
Lions	Penn State University—Mont Alto	Mont Alto, PA
Lions	Penn State University—New Kensington	New Kensington, PA
Lions	Penn State University—Schuylkill	Schuylkill Haven, PA

Senior Colleges and Universities—United States

Alphabetic Listing by Nickname/Mascot

Nickname/Mascot	Institution Name	Location
Lions	Penn State University—York	York, PA
Lions	Piedmont College	Demorest, GA
Lions	Southeastern Louisiana University	Hammond, LA
Lions	Southern Bible College	Houston, TX
Lions	Southwestern Assemblies of God University	Waxahachie, TX
Lions	St. Leo University	St. Leo, FL
Lions	Texas A & M University—Commerce	Commerce, TX
Lions	Trinity Bible College	Ellendale, ND
Lions	Vanguard University of Southern California	Costa Mesa, CA
Little Giants	Wabash College	Crawfordsville, IN
Lobos	New Mexico, University of	Albuquerque, NM
Lobos	Sul Ross State University	Alpine, TX
Loggers	Puget Sound, University of	Tacoma, WA
Longhorns	Texas, University of	Austin, TX
Lord Jeffs	Amherst College	Amherst, MA
Lords	Kenyon College	Gambier, OH
Lumberjacks	Humboldt State University	Arcata, CA
Lumberjacks	Northern Arizona University	Flagstaff, AZ
Lumberjacks	Northland College	Ashland, WI
Lumberjacks	Stephen F. Austin State University	Nacogdoches, TX
Lutes	Pacific Lutheran University	Tacoma, WA
Lynx	Lesley University	Cambridge, MA
Lynx	Rhodes College	Memphis, TN
Lyons	Mt. Holyoke College (Women)	South Hadley, MA
Lyons	Wheaton College	Norton, MA

M

Maccabees	Yeshiva University	New York, NY
Magicians	LeMoyne-Owen College	Memphis, TN
Majors	Millsaps College	Jackson, MS
Maple Leafs	Goshen College	Goshen, IN
Marauders	Central State University	Wilberforce, OH
Marauders	Mary, University of	Bismarck, ND
Marauders	Millersville University	Millersville, PA
Marauding Eagles	Marycrest International University	Davenport, IA
Mariners	Maine Maritime Academy	Castine, ME
Mariners	U.S. Merchant Marine Academy	Kings Point, NY
Marines	U.S. Marine Corps Academy	Quantico, VA
Maroon Tigers	Morehouse College	Atlanta, GA
Maroons	Chicago, University of	Chicago, IL

Senior Colleges and Universities—United States
Alphabetic Listing by Nickname/Mascot

Nickname/Mascot	Institution Name	Location
Maroons	Roanoke College	Salem, VA
Mastodons	Indiana University–Purdue University	Fort Wayne, IN
Matadors	Cal State University–Northridge	Northridge, CA
Mavericks	Medaille College	Buffalo, NY
Mavericks	Mesa State College	Grand Junction, CO
Mavericks	Minnesota State University—Mankato	Mankato, MN
Mavericks	National American University	Rapid City, SD
Mavericks	Nebraska–Omaha, University of	Omaha, NE
Mavericks	Texas–Arlington, University of	Arlington, TX
Mawrters	Bryn Mawr College (Women)	Bryn Mawr, PA
Mean Green	North Texas, University of	Denton, TX
Midshipmen	U.S. Naval Academy	Annapolis, MD
Mighty Macs	Immaculata College (Women)	Immaculata, PA
Mighty Oaks	Oakland City University	Oakland City, IN
Miners	Missouri–Rolla, University of	Rolla, MO
Miners	Texas–El Paso, University of (UTEP)	El Paso, TX
Minutemen	Heritage College	Orlando, FL
Minutemen	Massachusetts, University of	Amherst, MA
Missionaries	Whitman College	Walla Walla, WA
Moccasins	Florida Southern College	Lakeland, FL
Mocs	Tennessee–Chattanooga, University of	Chattanooga, TN
Monarchs	King's College	Wilkes-Barre, PA
Monarchs	Methodist College	Fayetteville, NC
Monarchs	Old Dominion University	Norfolk, VA
Monks	St. Joseph's College of Maine	Standish, ME
Moundbuilders	Southwestern College	Winfield, KS
Mountain Cats	Pittsburgh–Johnstown, University of	Johnstown, PA
Mountain Hawks	Lehigh University	Bethlehem, PA
Mountain Lions	Alliant International University	San Diego, CA
Mountain Lions	Colorado–Colorado Springs, University of	Colorado Springs, CO
Mountain Lions	Concord College	Athens, WV
Mountain Lions	Penn State University–Wilkes-Barre	Lehman, PA
Mountaineers	Appalachian State University	Boone, NC
Mountaineers	Berea College	Berea, KY
Mountaineers	Eastern Oregon University	La Grande, OR
Mountaineers	Mansfield University	Mansfield, PA
Mountaineers	Mt. St. Mary's College	Emmitsburg, MD
Mountaineers	Schreiner College	Kerrville, TX
Mountaineers	Southern Vermont College	Bennington, VT
Mountaineers	West Virginia, University of	Morgantown, WV

Alphabetic Listing by Nickname/Mascot

Nickname/Mascot	Institution Name	Location
Mountaineers	Western State College of Colorado	Gunnison, CO
Mounties	Mt. Aloysius College	Cresson, PA
Mounties	Mt. St. Clare College	Clinton, IA
Muleriders	Southern Arkansas University	Magnolia, AR
Mules/Jennies	Central Missouri State University	Warrensburg, MO
Mules	Muhlenburg College	Allentown, PA
Musketeers	Xavier University	Cincinnati, OH
Muskies	Lakeland College	Sheboygan, WI
Mustangs	Central Baptist College	Conway, AR
Mustangs	California Polytechnic University—SLO	San Luis Obispo, CA
Mustangs	Marygrove College	Detroit, MI
Mustangs	Master's College, The	Santa Clarita, CA
Mustangs	Morningside College	Sioux City, IA
Mustangs	Mt. Ida College	Newton Centre, MA
Mustangs	Mt. Mercy College	Cedar Rapids, IA
Mustangs	Southern Methodist University	Dallas, TX
Mustangs	Southwest, College of the	Hobbs, NM
Mustangs	Southwest State University	Marshall, MN
Mustangs	Villa Julie College	Stevenson, MD
Mustangs	Western New Mexico University	Silver City, NM

N

Nanooks	Alaska—Fairbanks, University of	Fairbanks, AK
Night Hawks	Thomas University	Thomasville, GA
Nighthawks	Newbury College	Brookline, MA
Nittany Lions	Penn State University	State College, PA
Nittany Lions	Penn State University—Beaver	Monaca, PA
Nittany Lions	Penn State University—Berks/Lehigh Val.	Reading, PA
Nittany Lions	Penn State University—Delaware	Media, PA
Nittany Lions	Penn State University—Hazleton	Hazleton, PA
Nittany Lions	Penn State University—Worthington/Scranton	Dunmore, PA
Nor'easters	New England, University of	Biddeford, ME
Norse	Luther College	Decorah, IA
Norse	Northern Kentucky University	Highland Heights, KY
Northern Lights/Skylights	Montana State University—Northern	Havre, MT

O

Oaks	Menlo College	Menlo Park, CA
Oilers	Findlay, University of	Findlay, OH
Oles or Lions	St. Olaf College	Northfield, MN

Senior Colleges and Universities—United States
Alphabetic Listing by Nickname/Mascot

Nickname/Mascot	Institution Name	Location
Orangemen	Syracuse University	Syracuse, NY
Orediggers	Colorado School of Mines	Golden, CO
Orediggers	Montana Tech of the University of Montana	Butte, MT
Ospreys	North Florida, University of	Jacksonville, FL
Ospreys	Stockton State College	Pomona, NJ
Otters	Cal State University–Monterey Bay	Seaside, CA
Owls	Florida Atlantic University	Boca Raton, FL
Owls	Hellenic College	Brookline, MA
Owls	Keene State College	Keene, NH
Owls	Kennesaw State University	Marietta, GA
Owls	Maine–Presque Isle, University of	Presque Isle, ME
Owls	Rice University	Houston, TX
Owls	Southern Connecticut State University	New Haven, CT
Owls	Temple University	Philadelphia, PA
Owls	Warren-Wilson College	Swannanoa, NC
Owls	Westfield State College	Westfield, MA
Owls	William Woods University	Fulton, MO

P

Nickname/Mascot	Institution Name	Location
Pacers	Marywood University	Scranton, PA
Pacers	S. Carolina–Aiken, University of	Aiken, SC
Palladins	Furman University	Greenville, SC
Panthers	Adelphi University	Garden City, NY
Panthers	Albany College of Pharmacy	Albany, NY
Panthers	Birmingham–Southern College	Birmingham, AL
Panthers	Chapman University	Orange, CA
Panthers	Claflin College	Orangeburg, SC
Panthers	Clark Atlanta University	Atlanta, GA
Panthers	Drury College	Springfield, MO
Panthers	Eastern Illinois University	Charleston, IL
Panthers	Ferrum College	Ferrum, VA
Panthers	Florida Institute of Technology	Melbourne, FL
Panthers	Georgia State University	Atlanta, GA
Panthers	Greenville College	Greenville, IL
Panthers	Hanover College	Hanover, IN
Panthers	High Point University	High Point, NC
Panthers	Kentucky Wesleyan College	Owensboro, KY
Panthers	La Grange College	La Grange, GA
Panthers	Middlebury College	Middlebury, VT
Panthers	Northern Iowa, University of	Cedar Falls, IA
Panthers	Ohio Dominican College	Columbus, OH

Senior Colleges and Universities—United States
Alphabetic Listing by Nickname/Mascot

Nickname/Mascot	Institution Name	Location
Panthers	Ohio University—Eastern Campus	St. Clairsville, OH
Panthers	Philander Smith College	Little Rock, AR
Panthers	Pittsburgh—Bradford, University of	Bradford, PA
Panthers	Pittsburgh, University of	Pittsburgh, PA
Panthers	Plymouth State College	Plymouth, NH
Panthers	Prairie View A & M University	Prairie View, TX
Panthers	Principia College	Elsah, IL
Panthers	SUNY—Old Westbury	Old Westbury, NY
Panthers	SUNY—Purchase College	Purchase, NY
Panthers	Virginia Union University	Richmond, VA
Panthers	Wisconsin—Milwaukee, University of	Milwaukee, WI
Panthers	York College	York, NE
Parsons	Nebraska Christian College	Norfolk, NE
Patriots	Arlington Baptist College	Arlington, TX
Patriots	Baptist Bible College	Springfield, MO
Patriots	Cumberland College	Williamsburg, KY
Patriots	Dallas Baptist University	Dallas, TX
Patriots	Francis Marion University	Florence, SC
Patriots	George Mason University	Fairfax, VA
Patriots	Texas—Tyler, University of	Tyler, TX
Patriots	Valley Forge Christian College	Phoenixville, PA
Peacocks/Peahens	St. Peter's College	Jersey City, NJ
Peacocks	Upper Iowa University	Fayette, IA
Pelicans	Spalding University	Louisville, KY
Penguins	Dominican University of California	San Rafael, CA
Penguins	Youngstown State University	Youngstown, OH
Penmen	New Hampshire College	Hooksett, NH
Pequots	Mitchell College	New London, CT
Phantoms	East-West University	Chicago, IL
Phoenix	Elon College	Elon College, NC
Phoenix	Wilson College (Women)	Chambersburg, PA
Phoenix	Wisconsin—Green Bay, University of	Green Bay, WI
Pilgrims	New England College	Henniker, NH
Pilots	Bethel College	Mishawaka, IN
Pilots	Louisiana State University—Shreveport	Shreveport, LA
Pilots	Portland, University of	Portland, OR
Pioneers	Alaska Pacific University	Anchorage, AK
Pioneers	Cal State University—Hayward	Hayward, CA
Pioneers	Carroll College	Waukesha, WI
Pioneers	Columbia Union College	Takoma Park, MD
Pioneers	Cooper Union	New York, NY

Senior Colleges and Universities—United States
Alphabetic Listing by Nickname/Mascot

Nickname/Mascot	Institution Name	Location
Pioneers	Denver, University of + Women's	
	College of the University of Denver	Denver, CO
Pioneers	Glenville State College	Glenville, WV
Pioneers	Grinnell College	Grinnell, IA
Pioneers	Lewis & Clark College	Portland, OR
Pioneers	Long Island University–CW Post Center	Brookville, NY
Pioneers	Malone College	Canton, OH
Pioneers	Marietta College	Marietta, OH
Pioneers	Mid-America Nazarene College	Olathe, KS
Pioneers	Northland Baptist Bible College	Dunbar, WI
Pioneers	Pacific Union College	Angwin, CA
Pioneers	Point Park College	Pittsburgh, PA
Pioneers	Sacred Heart University	Fairfield, CT
Pioneers	Smith College (Women)	Northampton, MA
Pioneers	Texas Women's University	Denton, TX
Pioneers	Transylvania University	Lexington, KY
Pioneers	Tusculum College	Greenville, TN
Pioneers	Utica College of Syracuse University	Utica, NY
Pioneers/Flying Queens	Wayland Baptist University	Plainview, TX
Pioneers	Wesleyan College (Women)	Macon, GA
Pioneers	Widener University	Chester, PA
Pioneers	William Paterson University	Wayne, NJ
Pioneers	Wisconsin–Platteville, University of	Platteville, WI
Pipers	Hamline University	St. Paul, MN
Pirates	Armstrong Atlantic State University	Savannah, GA
Pirates	East Carolina University	Greenville, NC
Pirates	Hampton University	Hampton, VA
Pirates	Park University	Parkville, MO
Pirates	Seton Hall University	South Orange, NJ
Pirates	Southwestern University	Georgetown, TX
Pirates	Whitworth College	Spokane, WA
Poets	Whittier College	Whittier, CA
Pointers	Wisconsin–Stevens Point, University of	Stevens Point, WI
Polar Bears	Bowdoin College	Brunswick, ME
Polar Bears	Ohio Northern University	Ada, OH
Pomeroys	St. Mary-of-the-Woods College (Women)	St. Mary-OTW, IN
Power Gulls	Endicott College	Beverly, MA
Prairie Fire	Knox College	Galesburg, IL
Prairie Stars	Illinois at Springfield, University of	Springfield, IL
Prairie Wolves	Nebraska Wesleyan University	Lincoln, NE
Preachers	Concordia Seminary	St. Louis, MO
Preachers	Lincoln Christian College & Seminary	Lincoln, IL

Senior Colleges and Universities—United States

Alphabetic Listing by Nickname/Mascot

Nickname/Mascot	Institution Name	Location
Preachers/Evangels	Johnson Bible College	Knoxville, TN
Presidents	Washington & Jefferson College	Washington, PA
Pride, The	Greensboro College	Greensboro, NC
Pride	Hofstra University	Hempstead, NY
Pride	Peace College (Women)	Raleigh, NC
Pride	Regis College (Women)	Weston, MA
Pride	Springfield College	Springfield, MA
Privateers	New Orleans, University of	New Orleans, LA
Privateers	SUNY—New York Maritime College	Ft. Schuyler, NY
Profs	Rowan University	Glassboro, NJ
Prophets	Oklahoma Baptist College & Institute	Oklahoma City, OK
Pumas	St. Joseph's College	Rensselaer, IN
Purple Aces	Evansville, University of	Evansville, IN
Purple Eagles	Niagara University	Niagara University, NY
Purple Knights	Bridgeport, University of	Bridgeport, CT
Purple Knights	St. Michael's College	Colchester, VT
Purple Pride	Nyack College	Nyack, NY
Purple Storm	Crown College	St. Bonifacius, MN

Q

Quakers	Earlham College	Richmond, IN
Quakers	Guilford College	Greensboro, NC
Quakers	Pennsylvania, University of	Philadelphia, PA
Quakers	Wilmington College	Wilmington, OH

R

Racers	Murray State University	Murray, KY
Raiders	Colgate University	Hamilton, NY
Raiders	Milwaukee School of Engineering	Milwaukee, WI
Raiders	Mt. Union College	Alliance, OH
Raiders	Rivier College	Nashua, NH
Raiders	Roberts Wesleyan College	Rochester, NY
Raiders	Southern Oregon University	Ashland, OR
Raiders	Wright State University	Dayton, OH
Railsplitters	Lincoln Memorial University	Harrogate, TN
Rainbow Warriors	Hawaii (Manoa), University of (Men's basketball)	Honolulu, HI
Rainbows/Rainbow Wahine	Hawaii (Manoa), University of	Honolulu, HI
Rajin' Cajuns	Louisiana at Lafayette, University of	Lafayette, LA

Senior Colleges and Universities—United States
Alphabetic Listing by Nickname/Mascot

Nickname/Mascot	Institution Name	Location
Ramblers	Loyola of Chicago University	Chicago, IL
Ramblers	Rosemont College (Women)	Rosemont, PA
Ramblin' Rams	Bluefield College	Bluefield, VA
Rams	Angelo State University	San Angelo, TX
Rams	Colorado State University	Ft. Collins, CO
Rams	Cornell College	Mount Vernon, IA
Rams	Fordham University	New York, NY
Rams	Framingham State College	Framingham, MA
Rams	Huston–Tillotson College	Austin, TX
Rams	Mobile, University of	Mobile, AL
Rams	North Central University	Minneapolis, MN
Rams	Philadelphia University	Philadelphia, PA
Rams	Rhode Island, University of	Kingston, RI
Rams	Shepherd College	Shepherdstown, WV
Rams	Suffolk University	Boston, MA
Rams	SUNY–Farmingdale	Farmingdale, NY
Rams	Temple Baptist College	Cincinnati, OH
Rams	Texas Wesleyan University	Ft. Worth, TX
Rams	Unity College	Unity, ME
Rams	Virginia Commonwealth University	Richmond, VA
Rams	Winston-Salem State University	Winston-Salem, NC
Rangers	Drew University	Madison, NJ
Rangers	Northwestern Oklahoma State University	Alva, OK
Rangers	Regis University	Denver, CO
Rangers	Wisconsin–Parkside, University of	Kenosha, WI
Rattlers	Florida A & M University	Tallahassee, FL
Rattlers	St. Mary's University	San Antonio, TX
Ravens	Anderson University	Anderson, IN
Ravens	Benedictine College	Atchison, KS
Ravens	Franklin Pierce College	Rindge, NH
Razorbacks	Arkansas, University of	Fayetteville, AR
Rebels	Maine–Augusta, University of	Augusta, ME
Rebels	Mississippi, University of	Oxford, MS
Red Devils	Dickinson College	Carlisle, PA
Red Devils	Eureka College	Eureka, IL
Red Dragons	SUNY–Cortland	Cortland, NY
Red Dragons	SUNY–Oneonta	Oneonta, NY
Red Flash	St. Francis College	Loretto, PA
Red Foxes	Marist College	Poughkeepsie, NY
Red Hawks	La Roche College	Pittsburgh, PA
Red Hawks	Montclair State University	Upper Montclair, NJ

Senior Colleges and Universities—United States

Alphabetic Listing by Nickname/Mascot

Nickname/Mascot	Institution Name	Location
Red Hawks	Ripon College	Ripon, WI
Red Raiders	Northwestern College	Orange City, IA
Red Raiders	Shippensburg University	Shippensburg, PA
Red Raiders	Texas Technical University	Lubbock, TX
Red Storm	St. John's University	Jamaica, NY
Redbirds	Illinois State University	Normal, IL
Reddies	Henderson State University	Arkadelphia, AR
RedHawks	Martin Methodist College	Pulaski, TN
RedHawks	Miami University	Oxford, OH
RedHawks	Indiana University—Northwest	Gary,IN
Redhawks	Seattle University	Seattle, WA
Redmen	Carthage College	Kenosha, WI
Redmen	Northeastern State University	Tahlequah, OK
Redmen	Rio Grande, University of	Rio Grande, OH
Regents	Rockford College	Rockford, IL
Retrievers	Maryland, Baltimore County, University of	Catonsville, MD
Revolution	Boston Baptist College	Boston, MA
Rifles	South Carolina—Spartanburg, University of	Spartanburg, SC
River Hawks	Massachusetts—Lowell, University of	Lowell, MA
Rivermen	Missouri—St. Louis, University of	St. Louis, MO
Roadrunners	Cal State University—Bakersfield	Bakersfield, CA
Roadrunners	Metropolitan State College	Denver, CO
Roadrunners	Ramapo College of New Jersey	Mahwah, NJ
Roadrunners	Texas—San Antonio, University of	San Antonio, TX
Roaring Lions	Penn State University—Fayette	Uniontown, PA
Rock, The	Slippery Rock University	Slippery Rock, PA
Rockets	Toledo, University of	Toledo, OH
Royal Crusaders	Crown College	Powell, TN
Royals	Bethel College and Seminary	St. Paul, MN
Royals	Eastern Mennonite University	Harrisonburg, VA
Royals	Grace University	Omaha, NE
Royals	Hope International University	Fullerton, CA
Royals	Minnesota Bible College	Rochester, MN
Royals	Pacific Christian College	Fullerton, CA
Royals	Queens College	Charlotte, NC
Royals	Scranton, University of	Scranton, PA
Royals	Warner Southern College	Lake Wales, FL
Runnin' Bulldogs	Gardner-Webb University	Boiling Springs, NC
Runnin' Bulldogs	Wilberforce University	Wilberforce, OH
Runnin' Rebels	Nevada—Las Vegas, University of (UNLV)	Las Vegas, NV

Senior Colleges and Universities—United States
Alphabetic Listing by Nickname/Mascot

Nickname/Mascot	Institution Name	Location
Runnin' Royals	California Christian College	Fresno, CA
Running Eagles	LIFE University	Marietta, GA

S

Nickname/Mascot	Institution Name	Location
Sabers	Barber-Scotia College	Concord, NC
Sabers	Southeastern Bible College	Birmingham, AL
Sabres	Marian College	Fond du Lac, WI
Sagehens	Pomona–Pitzer Colleges	Claremont, CA
Sailfish	Palm Beach Atlantic College	W. Palm Beach, FL
Saints	Aquinas College	Grand Rapids, MI
Saints	Emmanuel College	Boston, MA
Saints	Flagler College	St. Augustine, FL
Saints	Limestone College	Gaffney, SC
Saints	Hillsdale Free Will Baptist College	Moore, OK
Saints	Manna Bible Institute	Philadelphia, PA
Saints	Marymount College (Women)	Tarrytown, NY
Saints	Marymount University	Arlington, VA
Saints	Maryville University of St. Louis	St. Louis, MO
Saints	North Georgia College & State University	Dahlonega, GA
Saints	Notre Dame College	Manchester, NH
Saints	Presentation College	Aberdeen, SD
Saints	St. Francis, University of	Joliet, IL
Saints	St. Lawrence University	Canton, NY
Saints	St. Martin's College	Lacey, WA
Saints	St. Scholastica, College of	Duluth, MN
Saints	Siena College	Loudonville, NY
Saints	Siena Heights College	Adrian, MI
Saints	Steubenville University	Steubenville, OH
Saints	Thomas More College	Crestview Hills, KY
Salukis	Southern Illinois University–Carbondale	Carbondale, IL
Savages	Southeastern Oklahoma State University	Durant, OK
Saxons	Alfred University	Alfred, NY
Scarlet Hawks	Illinois Institute of Technology	Chicago, IL
Scarlet Knights	Arcadia College (formerly Beaver)	Glenside, PA
Scarlet Knights	Rutgers University	New Brunswick, NJ
Scarlet Raiders	Rutgers University–Newark	Newark, NJ
Scarlet Raptors	Rutgers University–Camden	Camden, NJ
Scorpions	Texas–Brownsville, University of and Texas Southmost College	Brownsville, TX
Scots	Alma College	Alma, MI

Senior Colleges and Universities—United States
Alphabetic Listing by Nickname/Mascot

Nickname/Mascot	Institution Name	Location
Scots	Covenant College	Lookout Mountain, GA
Scots	Macalester College	St. Paul, MN
Scots/Pipers	Lyon College	Batesville, AR
Scotties	Agnes Scott College (Women)	Atlanta/Decatur, GA
Screaming Eagles	(Si Tanka) Huron University	Huron, SD
Screaming Eagles	Southern Indiana, University of	Evansville, IN
Sea Gulls	Salisbury University	Salisbury, MD
Sea Warriors	Hawaii Pacific University	Honolulu, HI
Seagulls	Fort Lauderdale College	Fort Lauderdale, FL
Seahawks	N. Carolina—Wilmington, University of	Wilmington, NC
Seahawks	Northwood University	W. Palm Beach, FL
Seahawks	St. Mary's College of Maryland	St. Mary's City, MD
Seahawks	Salve Regina College	Newport, RI
Seahawks	Wagner College	Staten Island, NY
Seasiders	Brigham Young University—Hawaii	Laie, HI
Seawolves	Alaska—Anchorage, University of	Anchorage, AK
Seawolves	SUNY—Stony Brook	Stony Brook, NY
Seminoles	Florida State University	Tallahassee, FL
Senators	Auburn University—Montgomery	Montgomery, AL
Senators	Davis & Elkins College	Elkins, WV
Senators	Lander University	Greenwood, SC
Setters	Pace University	Pleasantville, NY
Sharks	Simmons College (Women)	Boston, MA
Shockers	Wichita State University	Wichita, KS
Shoremen	Washington College	Chestertown, MD
Silverswords	Chaminade University of Honolulu	Honolulu, HI
Skyhawks	Fort Lewis College	Durango, CO
Skyhawks	Tennessee—Martin, University of	Martin, TN
Soaring Eagles	Elmira College	Elmira, NY
Soldiers	St. Louis Christian College	Florissant, MO
Sooners	Oklahoma, University of	Norman, OK
Sound, The	Five Towns College	Dix Hills, NY
Spartans	Aurora University	Aurora, IL
Spartans	Cal State University—San Jose State	San Jose, CA
Spartans	Case Western Reserve University	Cleveland, OH
Spartans	Castleton State College	Castleton, VT
Spartans	Central Bible College	Springfield, MO
Spartans	D'Youville College	Buffalo, NY
Spartans	Dubuque, University of	Dubuque, IA
Spartans	Manchester College	N. Manchester, IN
Spartans	Michigan State University	East Lansing, MI
Spartans	Missouri Baptist College	St. Louis, MO

Senior Colleges and Universities—United States
Alphabetic Listing by Nickname/Mascot

Nickname/Mascot	Institution Name	Location
Spartans	Norfolk State University	Norfolk, VA
Spartans	North Carolina–Greensboro, University of	Greensboro, NC
Spartans	St. Thomas Aquinas College	Sparkill, NY
Spartans	Tampa, University of	Tampa, FL
Spartans	York College of Pennsylvania	York, PA
Spiders	Richmond, University of	Richmond, VA
Spires	St. Mary College	Leavenworth, KS
Spirit, The	Seton Hill College	Greensburg, PA
Spirits	Salem College (Women)	Winston-Salem, NC
Squirrels	Mary Baldwin College (Women)	Staunton, VA
Stags/Athenas	Claremont-Mudd-Scripps College	Claremont, CA
Stags	Fairfield University	Fairfield, CT
Stars	Dominican University	River Forest, IL
Stars	Oklahoma City University	Oklahoma City, OK
Stars	Stephens College (Women)	Columbia, MO
Statesmen	Bernard M. Baruch College of CUNY	New York, NY
Statesmen	Delta State University	Cleveland, MS
Statesmen	Hobart College	Geneva, NY
Statesmen	William Penn University	Oskaloosa, IA
Steers	Texas College	Tyler, TX
Storm	Lake Erie College	Painesville, OH
Storm	Simpson College	Indianola, IA
Stormy Petrels	Oglethorpe University	Atlanta, GA
Sun Devils	Arizona State University	Tempe, AZ
Sunbirds	Fresno Pacific College	Fresno, CA
Suns	Florida Christian College	Kissimmee, FL
Swedes	Bethany College	Lindsborg, KS
Swordsmen	LIFE Bible–East College	Christiansburg, VA
Swordsmen	Practical Biblical College	Johnson City, NY
Sycamores	Indiana State University–Terre Haute	Terra Haute, IN

T

Nickname/Mascot	Institution Name	Location
Tar Heels	North Carolina, University of	Chapel Hill, NC
Tars	Rollins College	Winter Park, FL
Tartans or Skibos	Carnegie-Mellon University	Pittsburgh, PA
Terrapins	Maryland, University of	College Park, MD
Terriers	Boston University	Boston, MA
Terriers	Hiram College	Hiram, OH
Terriers	St. Francis College	Brooklyn, NY
Terriers	Thomas College	Waterville, ME

Senior Colleges and Universities—United States

Alphabetic Listing by Nickname/Mascot

Nickname/Mascot	Institution Name	Location
Terriers	Wofford College	Spartanburg, SC
Texans	Tarleton State University	Stephenville, TX
Thorobreds	Kentucky State University	Frankfort, KY
Thoroughbreds	Skidmore College	Saratoga, NY
Threshers	Bethel College	N. Newton, KS
Thunder	Tri-State University	Angola, IN
Thunder	Wheaton College	Wheaton, IL
Thunderbirds	Cascade College	Portland, OR
Thunderbirds	Southern Utah University	Cedar City, UT
Thundering Herd	Marshall University	Huntington, WV
Thunderwolves	Southern Colorado, University of	Pueblo, CO
Tigers	Auburn University	Auburn, AL
Tigers	Benedict College	Columbia, SC
Tigers	Campbellsville University	Campbellsville, KY
Tigers	Central Christian College of Kansas	McPherson, KS
Tigers	Clemson University	Clemson, SC
Tigers	Colorado College	Colorado Springs,CO
Tigers	Dakota Wesleyan University	Mitchell, SD
Tigers	DePauw University	Greencastle, IN
Tigers	Doane College	Doane, NE
Tigers	East Central University	Ada, OK
Tigers	East Texas Baptist University	Marshall, TX
Tigers	Edward Waters College	Jacksonville, FL
Tigers	Fort Hays State University	Fort Hays, KS
Tigers	Georgetown College	Georgetown, KY
Tigers	Grace Bible College	Wyoming, MI
Tigers	Grambling State University	Grambling, LA
Tigers	Hampden-Sydney College	Farmville, VA
Tigers	Holy Family College	Philadelphia, PA
Tigers	Iowa Wesleyan College	Mt. Pleasant, IA
Tigers	Jackson State University	Jackson, MS
Tigers	Louisiana State University	Baton Rouge, LA
Tigers	Memphis University	Memphis, TN
Tigers	Missouri, University of	Columbia, MO
Tigers	Occidental College	Los Angeles, CA
Tigers	Olivet Nazarene University	Bourbonnais, IL
Tigers	Ouachita Baptist University	Arkadelphia, AR
Tigers	Pacific, University of the	Stockton, CA
Tigers	Paul Quinn College	Dallas, TX
Tigers	Princeton University	Princeton, NJ
Tigers	Rochester Institute of Technology (RIT)	Rochester, NY
Tigers	Salem-Teikyo University	Salem, WV
Tigers	Savannah State University	Savannah, GA

Senior Colleges and Universities—United States
Alphabetic Listing by Nickname/Mascot

Nickname/Mascot	Institution Name	Location
Tigers	South, University of the	Sewanee, TN
Tigers	St. Paul's College	Lawrenceville, VA
Tigers	Stillman College	Tuscaloosa, AL
Tigers	Strayer University	Washington, DC
Tigers	SUNY—Fashion Institute of Technology	New York, NY
Tigers	Tennessee State University	Nashville, TN
Tigers	Texas Southern University	Houston, TX
Tigers	Towson State University	Towson, MD
Tigers	Trinity College (Women)	Washington, DC
Tigers	Trinity College of Florida	New Port Richey, FL
Tigers	Trinity University	San Antonio, TX
Tigers	Voorhees College	Denmark, SC
Tigers	West Alabama, University of	Livingston, AL
Tigers	Wittenberg University	Springfield, OH
Timberwolves	Northwood University	Midland, MI
Titans	Cal State University—Fullerton	Fullerton, CA
Titans	Detroit Mercy, University of	Detroit, MI
Titans	Illinois Wesleyan University	Bloomington, IL
Titans	Indiana University—South Bend	South Bend, IN
Titans	Westminster College	New Wilmington, PA
Titans	Wisconsin—Oshkosh, University of	Oshkosh, WI
Tomcats/Ladycats	Thiel College	Greenville, PA
Tommies	St. Thomas, University of	St. Paul, MN
Toppers	Blue Mountain College (Women)	Blue Mountain, MS
Toreros	San Diego, University of	San Diego, CA
Tornados	Brevard College	Brevard, NC
Tornados	Concordia University at Austin	Austin, TX
Tornados	King College	Bristol, TN
Tornados	Talladega College	Talladega, AL
Toros	Cal State University—Dominguez Hills	Dominguez Hills, CA
Tracers	Ohio University—Zanesville	Zanesville, OH
Trailblazers	Massachusetts College of the Liberal Arts	North Adams, MA
Tribe	William & Mary, College of	Williamsburg, VA
Tritons	California—San Diego, University of	La Jolla, CA
Tritons	Eckerd College	St. Petersburg, FL
Trojans	Anderson University	Anderson, SC
Trojans	Arkansas—Little Rock, University of	Little Rock, AR
Trojans	Dakota State University	Madison, SD
Trojans	Hannibal—LaGrange College	Hannibal, MO
Trojans	Mt. Olive College	Mount Olive, NC
Trojans/Women of Troy	Southern Cal., University of (USC)	Los Angeles, CA

Senior Colleges and Universities—United States
Alphabetic Listing by Nickname/Mascot

Nickname/Mascot	Institution Name	Location
Trojans	Taylor University	Upland, IN
Trojans	Trevecca Nazarene University	Nashville, TN
Trojans	Trinity International University	Deerfield, IL
Trojans	Troy State University	Troy, AL
Trojans	Virginia State University	Petersburg, VA
Trolls	Trinity Christian College	Palos Heights, IL

U

Utes	Utah, University of	Salt Lake City, UT

V

V-Hawks	Viterbo College	La Crosse, WI
Valiants	Manhattanville College	Purchase, NY
Vandals	Idaho, University of	Moscow, ID
Vanguards	Simpson College	Redding, CA
Victors	Grand Rapids Bible/Music College	Grand Rapids, MI
Vikings/Vi Queens	Augustana College	Rock Island, IL
Vikings	Augustana College	Sioux Falls, SD
Vikings	Berry College	Mt. Berry, GA
Vikings	Bethany Lutheran College	Mankato, MN
Vikings	Cleveland State University	Cleveland, OH
Vikings	Dana College	Blair, NE
Vikings	Elizabeth City State University	Elizabeth City, NC
Vikings	Grand View College	Des Moines, IA
Vikings	Josephinum College	Columbus, OH
Vikings	Kendall College	Evanston, IL
Vikings	Lawrence University	Appleton, WI
Vikings	Missouri Valley College	Marshall, MO
Vikings	North Park University	Chicago, IL
Vikings	Portland State University	Portland, OR
Vikings	Salem State College	Salem, MA
Vikings	Valley City State University	Valley City, ND
Vikings	Western Washington University	Bellingham, WA
Violets	New York University (NYU)	New York, NY
Vixens	Sweet Briar College (Women)	Sweet Briar, VA
Volunteers	Tennessee, University of	Knoxville, TN
Vulcans	California University of Pennsylvania	California, PA
Vulcans	Hawaii—Hilo, University of	Hilo, HI

Senior Colleges and Universities—United States
Alphabetic Listing by Nickname/Mascot

Nickname/Mascot	Institution Name	Location

W

Nickname/Mascot	Institution Name	Location
Warhawks	Wisconsin–Whitewater, University of	Whitewater, WI
Warriors	American Indian College	Phoenix, AZ
Warriors	Appalachian Bible College	Bradley, WV
Warriors	Bacone College	Muskogee, OK
Warriors	Baptist Christian College	Shreveport, LA
Warriors	Cal State University–Stanislaus	Turlock, CA
Warriors	Calvary Bible College	Kansas City, MO
Warriors	Daemen College	Amherst, NY
Warriors	East Stroudsburg University	E. Stroudsburg, PA
Warriors	Eastern Connecticut State University	Willimantic, CT
Warriors	Hendrix College	Conway, AR
Warriors	Indiana Institute of Technology	Fort Wayne, IN
Warriors	Keuka College	Keuka Park, NY
Warriors	Lewis-Clark State College	Lewiston, ID
Warriors	LIFE Pacific College	San Dimas, CA
Warriors	Lycoming College	Williamsport, PA
Warriors	Merrimack College	N. Andover, MA
Warriors	Miami Christian College	Miami, FL
Warriors	Midland Lutheran College	Fremont, NE
Warriors	Rochester College	Rochester Hills, MI
Warriors	San Jose Christian College	San Jose, CA
Warriors	Southern Wesleyan University	Central, SC
Warriors	Sterling College	Sterling, KS
Warriors	Union College	Lincoln, NE
Warriors	United Wesleyan College	Allentown, PA
Warriors	Waldorf College	Forest City, IA
Warriors	Wayne State University	Detroit, MI
Warriors	Webber College	Babson Park, FL
Warriors	Western Baptist College	Salem, OR
Warriors	Westmont College	Santa Barbara, CA
Warriors	Winona State University	Winona, MN
Warriors	Wisconsin Lutheran College	Milwaukee, WI
Warriors	World Harvest Bible College	Columbus, OH
Wasps	Emory & Henry College	Emory, VA
Waves	Pepperdine University	Malibu, CA
Webbies or Clippers	Webb Institute	Glen Cove, LI, NY
White Mules	Colby College	Waterville, ME
Wildcats	Abilene Christian University	Abilene, TX
Wildcats	Arizona, University of	Tucson, AZ
Wildcats	Baker University	Baldwin, KS

Senior Colleges and Universities—United States
Alphabetic Listing by Nickname/Mascot

Nickname/Mascot	Institution Name	Location
Wildcats	Bay Path College (Women)	Longmeadow, MA
Wildcats	Bethel College	McKenzie, TN
Wildcats	Bethune-Cookman College	Daytona Beach, FL
Wildcats	Brewton-Parker College	Mt. Vernon, GA
Wildcats	Cal State University—Chico	Chico, CA
Wildcats	Cazenovia College	Cazenovia, NY
Wildcats	Central Washington University	Ellensburg, WA
Wildcats	Culver-Stockton College	Canton, MO
Wildcats	Davidson College	Davidson, NC
Wildcats	Fort Valley State University	Fort Valley, GA
Wildcats	Indiana Wesleyan University	Marion, IN
Wildcats	Johnson and Wales University	Charleston, SC
Wildcats	Johnson and Wales University	N. Miami, FL
Wildcats	Johnson and Wales University	Providence, RI
Wildcats	Kansas State University	Manhattan, KS
Wildcats	Kentucky, University of	Lexington, KY
Wildcats	Linfield College	McMinnville, OR
Wildcats	Louisiana College	Pineville, LA
Wildcats	New Hampshire, University of	Durham, NH
Wildcats	Northern Michigan University	Marquette, MI
Wildcats	Northwestern University	Evanston, IL
Wildcats	Pennsylvania College of Technology	Williamsport, PA
Wildcats	Randolph-Macon Women's College	Lynchburg, VA
Wildcats	St. Catherine (Women), College of	St. Paul, MN
Wildcats	SUNY—Institute of Technology at Utica/Rome	Utica, NY
Wildcats	Villanova University	Villanova, PA
Wildcats	Wayne State College	Wayne, NE
Wildcats	Weber State University	Ogden, UT
Wildcats	Wheelock College	Boston, MA
Wildcats	Wiley College	Marshall, TX
Wildcats	Wilmington College	New Castle, DE
Wolf Pack	Nevada, University of	Reno, NV
Wolfpack	Loyola University	New Orleans, LA
Wolfpack	North Carolina State University	Raleigh, NC
Wolfpack	Oak Hills Christian College	Bemidji, MN
Wolverines	Grove City College	Grove City, PA
Wolverines	Michigan, University of	Ann Arbor, MI
Wolverines	Morris Brown College	Atlanta, GA
Wolverines	Utah Valley State College	Orem, UT
Wolverines	Wesley College	Dover, DE

Senior Colleges and Universities—United States
Alphabetic Listing by Nickname/Mascot

Nickname/Mascot	Institution Name	Location
Wolves	Cheney University	Cheney, PA
Wolves	Michigan–Dearborn, University of	Dearborn, MI
Wolves	Northern State University	Aberdeen, SD
Wolves	Walla Walla College	College Place, OR
Wolves	Western Oregon University	Monmouth, OR
Wonder Boys/Golden Suns	Arkansas Technical University	Russellville, AR

Y

Nickname/Mascot	Institution Name	Location
Yellow Jackets	Allen University	Columbia, SC
Yellow Jackets	American International College	Springfield, MA
Yellow Jackets	Baldwin-Wallace College	Berea, OH
Yellow Jackets	Black Hills State University	Spearfish, ND
Yellow Jackets	Cedarville University	Cedarville, OH
Yellow Jackets	Defiance College	Defiance, OH
Yellow Jackets	Georgia Institute of Technology (Georgia Tech)	Atlanta, GA
Yellow Jackets	Howard Payne University	Brownwood, TX
Yellow Jackets	New York City Technology College of CUNY	Brooklyn, NY
Yellow Jackets	Randolph-Macon College	Ashland, VA
Yellow Jackets	West Virginia State College	Institute, WV
Yellowjackets	Graceland University	Lamoni, IA
YellowJackets	LeTourneau University	Longview, TX
Yellowjackets	Montana State University–Billings	Billings, MT
Yellowjackets	Rochester, University of	Rochester, NY
Yellowjackets	Waynesburg College	Waynesburg, PA
Yellowjackets	Wisconsin–Superior, University of	Superior, WI
Yeomen	Oberlin College	Oberlin, OH

Z

Nickname/Mascot	Institution Name	Location
Zips	Akron, University of	Akron, OH

Did you know. . .

that with the exception of the three military academies, Western Illinois University is the only non-military institution in the nation to have its nickname, "The Fighting Leathernecks," attributed to a branch of the military service. In 1927, Ray "Rock" Hanson, a Marine veteran of WWI and WWII, and the athletic director, received permission from the U.S. Navy Department to use the Marine's official seal, their mascot (Bulldog), along with their nickname.

In 1977, a county-wide nickname contest was held to come up with a nickname for the women's teams. The women athletes and coaches voted for the nickname "Westerwinds."

Part 3

Junior and Community Colleges

United States

Alphabetic Listing by Institution

Did you know. . .

that the Gorlok is Webster University's school mascot. The myth says that the creature was designed by Webster staff and students. It is reported to have the paws of a speeding cheetah, horns of a fierce buffalo, and the face of a dependable St. Bernard. The myth of the Gorlok "embodies the highest standards of speed, agility, and stamina in an atmosphere of fairness and good conduct."

(Tom Hart, Director of Athletics)

Junior and Community Colleges—United States
Alphabetic Listing by Institution

Institution Name	Location	Nickname/Mascot

A

Institution Name	Location	Nickname/Mascot
Abraham Baldwin Agricultural College	Tifton, GA	Golden Stallions/ Golden Fillies
Adirondack Community College–SUNY	Queensbury, NY	Mountaineers
Aiken Technical College	Aiken, SC	Knights
Alabama Southern Community College	Monroeville, AL	Eagles
Alameda, College of	Alameda, CA	Cougars
Alfred State College of Technology–SUNY	Alfred, NY	Pioneers
Allan Hancock College	Santa Maria, CA	Bulldogs
Allegheny College of Maryland	Cumberland, MD	Trojans
Allegheny Cnty–Allegheny, Com. Col. of	Pittsburgh, PA	Cougars
Allegheny Cnty–Boyce, Com. Col. of	Monroeville, PA	Saints
Allegheny Cnty–South, Com. Col. of	West Mifflin, PA	Tigers
Allen County Community College	Iola, KS	Red Devils
Alpena Community College	Alpena, MI	Lumberjacks
Alvin Community College	Alvin, TX	Dolphins
American Educ. Complex Junior College	Killeen, TX	Golden Eagles
American River College	Sacramento, CA	Beavers
Ancilla College	Donaldson, IN	Chargers
Andrew College	Cuthbert, GA	Fighting Tigers
Angelina College	Lufkin, TX	Roadrunners
Anne Arundel Community College	Arnold, MD	Pioneers
Anoka-Ramsey Community College	Coon Rapids, MN	Golden Rams
Antelope Valley College	Lancaster, CA	Marauders
Aquinas Junior College	Nashville, TN	Cavaliers
Arizona Western College	Yuma, AZ	Matadors
Arkansas–Fort Smith, University of	Fort Smith, AR	Lions
Arkansas State Univ.–Mountain Home	Mountain Home, AR	Trailblazers
Asheville–Buncombe Tech Junior College	Asheville, NC	Atomics
Atlanta Area Technical College	Atlanta, GA	Flames
Atlanta Metropolitan College	Atlanta, GA	Red Eyed Panthers
Atlantic Cape Community College	Mays Landing, NJ	Buccaneers
Augusta Technical College	Atlanta, GA	**** (Golf Only)

B

Institution Name	Location	Nickname/Mascot
Bakersfield College	Bakersfield, CA	Renegades
Baltimore City Community College	Baltimore, MD	Red Devils
Baltimore Cnty–Catonsville, Com. Col. of	Catonsville, MD	Cardinals
Baltimore Cnty–Dundalk, Com. Col. of	Baltimore, MD	Lions
Baltimore Cnty–Essex, Com. College of	Baltimore, MD	Knights
Barstow College	Barstow, CA	Vikings
Barton County Community College	Great Bend, KS	Cougars

Junior and Community Colleges—United States
Alphabetic Listing by Institution

Institution Name	Location	Nickname/Mascot
Bay De Noc Community College	Escanaba, MI	Norsemen
Beaver County, Community College of	Monaca, PA	Titans
Becker College	Leicester, MA	Hawks
Bellevue Community College	Bellevue, WA	Helmsmen
Bergen Community College	Paramus, NJ	Bulldogs
Berkshire Community College	Pittsfield, MA	Falcons
Bethany Lutheran College	Mankato, MN	Vikings
Bevill State Community College	Sumiton, AL	Bears
Bevill State Community College—Fayette	Fayette, AL	Bears
Big Bend Community College	Moses Lake, WA	Vikings
Bishop State Community College	Mobile, AL	Wildcats
Bismarck State College	Bismarck, ND	Mystics
Black Hawk College	Moline, IL	Braves
Black Hawk College—East	Kewanee, IL	Warriors
Blanton Junior College	Asheville, NC	Raiders
Blinn College	Brenham, TX	Buccaneers
Blue Mountain Community College	Pendleton, OR	Timberwolves
Borough of Manhattan Com. Col.—CUNY	New York, NY	Panthers
Bossier Parish Community College	Bossier City, LA	Cavaliers
Brainerd Community College	Brainerd, MN	Raiders
Brandywine College	Wilmington, DE	Patriots
Brevard Community College	Cocoa, FL	Titans
Brevard College	Brevard, NC	Tornadoes
Brewer State Junior College	Fayette, AL	Bears
Briarcliffe College	Bethpage, NY	Seahawks
Bristol Community College	Fall River, MA	Knights
Bronx Community College—CUNY	Bronx, NY	Broncos
Brookdale Community College	Lincroft, NJ	Jersey Blues
Brookhaven College	Farmers Branch, TX	Bears
Broome Community College—SUNY	Binghamton, NY	Hornets
Broward Community College	Ft. Lauderdale, FL	Seahawks
Broward Com. College—Central Campus	Davie, FL	Seahawks
Broward Com. College—North Campus	Coconut Creek, FL	Seahawks
Brown Mackie College, The	Salina, KS	Lions
Brunswick Community College	Supply, NC	Dolphins
Bryant & Stratton	Syracuse, NY	Bobcats
Bucks County Community College	Newtown, PA	Centurions
Bunker Hill Community College	Charlestown, MA	Bulldogs
Burlington County College	Pemberton, NJ	Barons
Butler County Community College	Butler, PA	Pioneers
Butler County Community College	El Dorado, KS	Grizzlies
Butte College	Oroville, CA	Roadrunners

Junior and Community Colleges—United States
Alphabetic Listing by Institution

Institution Name	Location	Nickname/Mascot
C		
Cabrillo College	Aptos, CA	Seahawks
Caldwell Com. Col. & Tech. Institute	Hudson, NC	Cobras
Camden County College	Blackwood, NJ	Cougars
Canada College	Redwood City, CA	Colts
Canton College of Technology–SUNY	Canton, NY	Northstars
Canyons, College of the	Valencia, CA	Cougars
Cape Cod Community College	Barnstable, MA	Helmsmen
Cape Fear Community College	Wilmington, NC	Sea Devils
Capital Community College	Hartford, CT	Commodores
Carl Albert State College	Poteau, OH	Vikings
Carl Sandburg College	Galesburg, IL	Chargers
Casper College	Casper, WY	Thunderbirds (T-Birds)
Catawba Valley Community College	Hickory, NC	Buccaneers
Cayuga Community College–SUNY	Auburn, NY	Spartans
Cecil Community College	North East, MD	Seahawks
Cedar Valley College	Lancaster, TX	Suns
Central Alabama Community College	Alexander City, AL	Trojans
Central Arizona College	Coolidge, AZ	Vaqueros
Central Baptist College	Conway, AR	Mustangs
Central Carolina Community College	Sanford, NC	Cougars
Central College	McPherson, KS	Tigers
Central Community College	Hastings, NE	Rams
Central Community College–Platte	Columbus, NE	Raiders
Central Florida Community College	Ocala, FL	Patriots
Central Lakes College–Brainerd	Brainerd, MN	Raiders
Central Maine Technical College	Auburn, ME	Mustangs
Central Oregon Community College	Bend, OR	Bobcats
Central Piedmont Community College	Charlotte, NC	Tigers
Central Wyoming College	Riverton, WY	Rustlers
Centralia College	Centralia, WA	Trailblazers
Cerritos College	Norwalk, CA	Falcons
Cerro Coso Community College	Ridgecrest, CA	Coyotes
Chabot College	Hayward, CA	Gladiators
Chaffey College	Rancho Cucamonga, CA	Panthers
Champlain College	Burlington, VT	Beavers
Chandler–Gilbert Community College	Chandler, AZ	Coyotes
Chattahoochee Valley Community College	Phenix City, AL	Pirates
Chattanooga State Tech. Com. College	Chattanooga, TN	Tigers
Chemeketa Community College	Salem, OR	Storm
Chesapeake College	Wye Mills, MD	Skipjacks
Chipola Community College	Marianna, FL	Indians
Chowan College	Murfreesboro, TN	Braves

Junior and Community Colleges—United States
Alphabetic Listing by Institution

Institution Name	Location	Nickname/Mascot
Cincinnati State Technical & Com. College	Cincinnati, OH	Surge
Cisco Junior College	Cisco, TX	Wranglers
Citrus College	Glendora, CA	Owls
Clackamas Community College	Oregon City, OR	Cougars
Clarendon College	Clarendon, TX	Bulldogs
Clark College	Vancouver, WA	Penguins
Clark State Community College	Springfield, OH	Eagles
Clarke College	Newton, MS	Panthers
Cleveland State Community College	Cleveland, TN	Cougars
Clinton Community College	Clinton, IA	Huskers
Clinton Community College—SUNY	Plattsburgh, NY	Cougars
Clinton Junior College	Rock Hill, SC	Bears
Cloud County Community College	Concordia, KS	Thunderbirds
Coahoma Junior College	Clarksdale, MS	Tigers
Coastal Carolina Community College	Jacksonville, NC	Cougars
Coastal Georgia Community College	Brunswick, GA	Mariners
Cobleskill College of Ag. & Tech.—SUNY	Cobleskill, NY	Fighting Tigers
Cochise College	Douglas, AZ	Apaches
Coffeyville Community College	Coffeyville, KS	Red Ravens
Colby Community College	Colby, KS	Trojans
Collin County Community College	Plano, TX	Express
Colorado Northwestern Community College	Rangeley, CO	Spartans
Columbia Basin Community College	Pasco, WA	Hawks
Columbia College	Columbia, CA	Claim Jumpers
Columbia State Community College	Columbia, TN	Chargers
Columbia-Greene Com. College (SUNY)	Hudson, NY	Twins
Columbus State Community College	Columbus, OH	Cougars
Compton Community College	Compton, CA	Tartars
Concordia College—Selma	Selma, AL	Hornets
Connecticut—Avery Point, University of	Groton, CT	Pointers
Connors State College	Warner, OK	Cowboys
Contra Costa College	San Pablo, CA	Comets
Cooke County College	Gainesville, TX	Lions
Copiah—Lincoln Community College	Wesson, MS	Wolves
Corning Community College—SUNY	Corning, NY	Red Barons
Cosumnes River College	Sacramento, CA	Hawks
Cowley College	Arkansas City, KS	Tigers
Craven Community College	New Bern, NC	Panthers
Crowder College	Neosho, MO	Roughriders
Crowley's Ridge College	Paragould, AK	Pioneers
Cuesta College	San Luis Obispo,CA	Cougars
Cumberland County College	Vineland, NJ	Dukes
Cuyahoga Community College	Highland Hills, OH	Challengers

Junior and Community Colleges—United States
Alphabetic Listing by Institution

Institution Name	Location	Nickname/Mascot
Cuyamaca College	El Cajon, CA	Coyotes
Cypress College	Cypress, CA	Chargers

D

Dakota County Technical College	Rosemount, MN	Blue Knights
Danville Area Community College	Danville, IL	Jaguars
Darton College	Albany, GA	Cavaliers
Davenport College	Grand Rapids, MI	Panthers
Davidson County Community College	Lexington, NC	Cavaliers
Dawson Community College	Glendive, MT	Buccaneers
Daytona Beach Community College	Daytona Beach, FL	Falcons
De Anza College	Cupertino, CA	Dons
Dean College	Franklin, MA	Bulldogs
DeKalb College	Dunwoody, GA	Patriots
Delaware County Community College	Media, PA	Phantoms
Delaware Technical & Commmunity College (Stanton-Wilmington)	Newark, DE	Spirit
Delaware Technical & Community College (Terry)	Dover, DE	Skeeters
Delaware Technical & Community College (Owens)	Georgetown, DE	Roadrunners
Delgado Community College	New Orleans, LA	Dolphins
Delhi College of Technology—SUNY	Delhi, NY	Broncos
Delta College	University Center, MI	Pioneers
Des Moines Area Community College	Boone, IA	Bears
Desert, College of the	Palm Desert, CA	Roadrunners
Diablo Valley College	Pleasant Hill, CA	Vikings
Diné College	Tsaile, AZ	Warriors
Dixie State College of Utah	St. George, UT	Rebels
Dodge City Community College	Dodge City, KS	Conquistadors
Dull Knife Memorial College	Lame Deer, MT	Warriors
Dundalk Community College	Baltimore, MD	Lions
DuPage, College of	Glen Ellyn, IL	Chaparrals
Dutchess Community College—SUNY	Poughkeepsie, NY	Falcons
Dyersburg State Community College	Dyersburg, TN	Eagles

E

East Central College	Union, MO	Rebels
East Central Community College	Decatur, MS	Warriors
East Los Angeles College	Monterey Park, CA	Huskies
East Mississippi Community College	Scooba, MS	Lions

Junior and Community Colleges—United States
Alphabetic Listing by Institution

Institution Name	Location	Nickname/Mascot
Eastern Arizona College	Thatcher, AZ	Gilamonsters
Eastern Maine Technical College	Bangor, ME	Golden Eagles
Eastern Oklahoma State College	Wilburton, OK	Mountaineers
Eastern Utah, College of	Price, UT	Golden Eagles
Eastern Wyoming College	Torrington, WY	Lancers
Eastfield College	Mesquite, TX	Harvesters
Edison Community College	Fort Myers, FL	Buccaneers
Edison Community College	Piqua, OH	Chargers
Edmonds Community College	Lynwood, WA	Tritons
Edward Williams Junior College	Hackensack, NJ	Knights
El Camino College	Torrance, CA	Warriors
El Paso Community College	El Paso, TX	Tejanos
Elgin Community College	Elgin, IL	Spartans
Ellsworth Community College	Iowa Falls, IA	Panthers
Enterprise State Junior College	Enterprise, AL	Boll Weevils
Erie Community College—SUNY	Buffalo, NY	Kats
Essex Community College	Baltimore, MD	Knights
Essex County College	Newark, NJ	Wolverines
Everett Community College	Everett, WA	Trojans

F

Institution Name	Location	Nickname/Mascot
Faulkner State Community College	Bay Minette, AL	Sun Chiefs
Feather River College	Quincy, CA	Golden Eagles
Fergus Falls Community College	Fergus Falls, MN	Spartans
Finger Lakes Community College	Canadaigua, NY	Lakers
Flathead Valley Community College	Kalispell, MT	Eagles
Florida Community College at Jacksonville	Jacksonville, FL	Stars
Florida College	Temple Terrace, FL	Falcons
Floyd College	Rome, GA	Chargers
Foothill College	Los Altos Hills, CA	Owls
Forsyth Technical Community College	Winston-Salem, NC	Tigers
Fort Scott Community College	Fort Scott, KS	Greyhounds
Frank Phillips College	Borger, TX	Plainsmen
Frederick Community College	Frederick, MD	Cougars
Fresno City College	Fresno, CA	Rams
Fullerton College	Fullerton, CA	Hornets
Fulton—Montgomery Com. College (SUNY)	Johnstown, NY	Raiders

G

Institution Name	Location	Nickname/Mascot
Gadsden State Community College	Gadsden, AL	Cardinals
Galveston College	Galveston, TX	Whitecaps

Junior and Community Colleges—United States
Alphabetic Listing by Institution

Institution Name	Location	Nickname/Mascot
Garden City Community College	Garden City, KS	Broncbusters
Garland County Community College	Hot Springs, AR	Lakers
Garrett Community College	McHenry, MD	Lakers
GateWay Community College	Phoenix, AZ	Geckos
Gateway Community College	New Haven, CT	Lions
Gavilan College	Gilroy, CA	Rams
Genesee Community College–SUNY	Batavia, NY	Cougars
George C. Wallace State Com. College	Dothan, AL	Governors
Georgia Military College	Milledgeville, GA	Bulldogs
Georgia Perimeter College	Dunwoody, GA	Jaguars
Glen Oaks Community College	Centreville, MI	Vikings
Glendale Community College	Glendale, AZ	Gauchos
Glendale College	Glendale, CA	Vaqueros
Globe Institute of Technology	New York, NY	Knights
Gloucester County College	Sewell, NJ	Roadrunners
Gogebic Community College	Ironwood, MI	Samsons
Golden West College	Huntington Beach, CA	Rustlers
Gordon College	Barnesville, GA	Highlanders
Grand Rapids Community College	Grand Rapids, MI	Raiders
Grays Harbor College	Aberdeen, WA	Chokers
Grayson County College	Denison, TX	Vikings
Green River Community College	Auburn, WA	Gators
Grossmont College	El Cajon, CA	Griffins
Gulf Coast Community College	Panama City, FL	Commodores

H

Institution Name	Location	Nickname/Mascot
Hagerstown Community College	Hagerstown, MD	Hawks
Harford Community College	Bel Air, MD	Fighting Owls
Harper College	Palatine, IL	Hawks
Hartnell Community College	Salinas, CA	Panthers
Henry Ford Community College	Dearborn, MI	Hawks
Herkimer County Community College	Herkimer, NY	Generals
Hesser College	Manchester, NH	Blue Devils
Hesston College	Hesston, KS	Larks
Hibbing Community College	Hibbing, MN	Cardinals
Highland Community College	Freeport, IL	Cougars
Highland Community College	Highland, KS	Scotties
Highline Community College	Des Moines, WA	Thunderbirds
Hill College	Hillsboro, TX	Rebels
Hillsborough Community College	Tampa, FL	Hawks
Hinds Community College	Raymond, MS	Eagles
Hiwassee College	Madisonville, TN	Tigers

Junior and Community Colleges—United States
Alphabetic Listing by Institution

Institution Name	Location	Nickname/Mascot
Holmes Community College	Goodman, MS	Bulldogs
Holyoke Community College	Holyoke, MA	Cougars
Housatonic Community College	Bridgeport, CT	Hawks
Howard Community College	Columbia, MD	Dragons
Howard College	Big Spring, TX	Hawks
Hudson Valley Community College—SUNY	Troy, NY	Vikings
Hutchison Community College	Hutchison, KS	Blue Dragons

I

Illinois Central College	East Peoria, IL	Cougars
Illinois Valley Community College	Oglesby, IL	Eagles
Imperial Valley College	Imperial, CA	Arabs
Independence Community College	Independence, KS	Pirates
Indian Hills Com. College—Centerville	Centerville, IA	Falcons
Indian Hills Com. College—Ottumwa	Ottumwa, IA	Warriors
Indian River Community College	Ft. Pierce, FL	Pioneers
Iowa Central Community College	Fort Dodge, IA	Tritons
Iowa Lakes Community College	Estherville, IA	Lakers
Iowa Western Community College	Council Bluffs, IA	Reivers
Irvine Valley College	Irvine, CA	Lasers
Itasca Community College	Grand Rapids, MN	Vikings
Itawamba Community College	Fulton, MS	Indians

J

Jackson State Community College	Jackson, TN	Generals
Jacksonville College	Jacksonville, TX	Jaguars
James Sprunt Technical College	Kenansville, NC	Spartans
Jamestown Community College—SUNY	Jamestown, NY	Jayhawks
Jamestown Com. College, Olean—SUNY	Olean, NY	Jaguars
Jefferson Community College—SUNY	Watertown, NY	Cannoneers
Jefferson College	Hillsboro, MO	Vikings
Jefferson Davis Community College	Brewton, AL	Warhawks
Jefferson State Community College	Birmingham, AL	Pioneers
John A. Logan College	Carterville, IL	Volunteers
John Wood Community College	Quincy, IL	Trail Blazers
Johnson County Community College	Overland Park, KS	Cavaliers
Joliet Junior College	Joliet, IL	Wolves
Jones County Junior College	Ellisville, MS	Bobcats

Junior and Community Colleges—United States
Alphabetic Listing by Institution

Institution Name	Location	Nickname/Mascot

K

Institution Name	Location	Nickname/Mascot
Kalamazoo Valley Community College	Kalamazoo, MI	Cougars
Kankakee Community College	Kankakee, IL	Cavaliers
Kansas City Kansas Community College	Kansas City, KS	Blue Devils
Kaskaskia College	Centralia, IL	Blue Devils/Blue Angels
Kellogg Community College	Battle Creek, MI	Bruins
Kemper Military School and College	Boonville, MO	Yellowjackets
Kennedy-King College (Com. College)	Chicago, IL	Statesmen
Kent State University	East Liverpool, OH	Bridgers
Kent State University—Ashtabula	Ashtabula, OH	Vikings
Kent State University—Salem	Salem, OH	Cougars
Kent State University—Trumbull	Warren, OH	Titans
Kent State University—Tuscarawas	New Phila., OH	Kubs
Keystone College	LaPlume, PA	Giants
Kilgore College	Kilgore, TX	Rangers
Kingsborough Community College—CUNY	Brooklyn, NY	Wave, The
Kirkwood Community College	Cedar Rapids, IA	Eagles
Kirtland Community College	Roscommon, MI	Firebirds
Kishwaukee College	Malta, IL	Kougars

L

Institution Name	Location	Nickname/Mascot
Labette Community College	Parsons, KS	Cardinals
Lackawanna College	Scranton, PA	Falcons
Lake-Sumter Community College	Leesburg, FL	Lakers
Lake City Community College	Lake City, FL	Timberwolves
Lake County, College of	Grayslake, IL	Lancers
Lake Land College	Mattoon, IL	Lakers
Lake Michigan College	Benton Harbor, MI	Indians
Lake Region State College	Devils Lake, ND	Royals
Lakeland Community College	Kirtland, OH	Lakers
Lamar Community College	Lamar, CO	Antelopes
Lane Community College	Eugene, OR	Titans
Laney College	Oakland, CA	Eagles
Lansing Community College	Lansing, MI	Stars
Laramie County Community College	Cheyenne, WY	Golden Eagles
Laredo Community College	Laredo, TX	Palominos
Las Positas College	Livermore, CA	Hawks
Lassen Community College	Susanville, CA	Cougars
Lawson State Community College	Birmingham, AL	Cougars
Lee College	Baytown, TX	Runnin' Rebels
Lees Junior College	Jackson, KY	Generals

Junior and Community Colleges—United States
Alphabetic Listing by Institution

Institution Name	Location	Nickname/Mascot
Lehigh Carbon Community College	Schnecksville, PA	Cougars
Lenoir Community College	Kinston, NC	Lancers
Lewis & Clark Community College	Godfrey, IL	Trailblazers
Lincoln College	Lincoln, IL	Lynx
Lincoln Land Community College	Springfield, IL	Loggers
Lincoln School of Commerce	Lincoln, NE	Aliens
Lincoln Trail College	Robinson, IL	Statesmen
Linn State Technical College	Linn, MO	Eagles
Linn-Benton Community College	Albany, OR	Roadrunners
Lon Morris College	Jacksonville, TX	Bearcats
Long Beach City College	Long Beach, CA	Vikings
Longview Community College	Lee's Summit, MO	Lakers
Los Angeles City College	Los Angeles, CA	Cubs
Los Angeles Harbor College	Wilmington, CA	Seahawks
Los Angeles Mission College	Sylmar, CA	Free Spirit
Los Angeles Pierce College	Woodland Hills, CA	Brahmas
Los Angeles Southwest College	Los Angeles, CA	Cougars
Los Angeles Trade-Technical College	Los Angeles, CA	Beavers
Los Angeles Valley College	Van Nuys, CA	Monarchs
Los Medanos College	Pittsburg, CA	Mustangs
Louisburg College	Louisburg, NC	Hurricanes
Louisiana State University—Eunice	Eunice, LA	Bengals
Lower Columbia College	Longview, WA	Red Devils
Lurleen B. Wallace Junior College	Andalusia, AL	Saints
Luzerne County Community College	Nanticoke, PA	Trailblazers

M

Institution Name	Location	Nickname/Mascot
Macomb Community College	Warren, MI	Monarchs
Macon Junior College	Macon, GA	Roadrunners
Madison Area Technical College	Madison, WI	WolfPack
Malcolm X College—City College of Chicago	Chicago, IL	Hawks
Manatee Community College	Bradenton, FL	Lancers
Manchester Community College	Manchester, CT	Cougars
Maple Woods Community College	Kansas City, MO	Centaurs
Marin, College of	Kentfield, CA	Mariners
Marion Military Institute	Marion, AL	Tigers
Marshalltown Community College	Marshalltown, IA	Tigers
Mary Holmes College	West Point, MS	Eagles
Marymount College	Rancho Palos Verdes,CA	Mariners
Massachusetts Bay Community College	Wellesley Hills, MA	Buccaneers
Massasoit Community College	Brockton, MA	Warriors

Junior and Community Colleges—United States
Alphabetic Listing by Institution

Institution Name	Location	Nickname/Mascot
McHenry County College	Crystal Lake, IL	Fighting Scots
McLennan Community College	Waco, TX	Highlanders/Highlassies
Mendocino College	Ukiah, CA	Eagles
Merced College	Merced, CA	Blue Devils
Mercer County Community College	Trenton, NJ	Vikings
Mercyhurst College—North East	North East, PA	Saints
Meridian Community College	Meridian, MS	Eagles
Merritt College	Oakland, CA	Thunderbirds
Mesa Community College	Mesa, AZ	Thunderbirds
Mesabi Range Com. & Technical College	Virginia, MN	Norse
Miami University—Middletown	Middletown, OH	ThunderHawks
Miami-Dade Community College	Miami, FL	Sharks
Mid-Plains Com. Col. Area—McCook	McCook, NE	Indians
Mid-Plains Com. Col. Area—North Platte	North Platte, NE	Knights
Mid-State Technical College	Wisconsin Rapids, WI	Cougars
Middle Georgia College	Cochran, GA	Warriors
Middlesex Community College	Middletown, CT	Flying Horsemen
Middlesex County College	Edison, NJ	Colts
Midland College	Midland, TX	Chaparrals
Miles Community College	Miles City, MT	Pioneers
Milwaukee Area Technical College	Milwaukee, WI	Stormers
Mineral Area College	Park Hills, MO	Cardinals
Minneapolis Com. & Technical College	Minneapolis, MN	Marauders
Minnesota West Com. & Tech. College	Worthington, MN	Bluejays
Minot State University—Bottineau	Bottineau, ND	Lumberjacks
MiraCosta College	Oceanside, CA	Spartans
Miramar College	San Diego, CA	Jets
Mission College	Santa Clara, CA	Saints
Mississippi County Community College	Blytheville, AR	Suns
Mississippi Delta Community College	Moorhead, MS	Trojans
Mississippi Gulf Coast Community College	Perkinston, MS	Bulldogs
Mitchell Community College	Statesville, NC	Mavericks
Moberly Area Community College	Moberly, MO	Greyhounds
Modesto Junior College	Modesto, CA	Pirates
Mohawk Valley Community College	Utica, NY	Hawks
Monroe College	Bronx, NY	Mustangs
Monroe Community College—SUNY	Rochester, NY	Tribunes
Monterey Peninsula College	Monterey, CA	Lobos
Montgomery College—Germantown	Germantown, MD	Gryphons
Montgomery College—Rockville	Rockville, MD	Knights
Montgomery College—Takoma Park	Takoma Park, MD	Falcons
Moorpark College	Moorpark, CA	Raiders

Junior and Community Colleges—United States
Alphabetic Listing by Institution

Institution Name	Location	Nickname/Mascot
Moraine Park Technical Institute	Fond du Lac, WI	Panthers
Moraine Valley Community College	Palos Hills, IL	Cyclones
Morris, County College of	Randolph, NJ	Titans
Morrisville College of Ag. & Tech.–SUNY	Morrisville, NY	Mustangs
Morton College	Cicero, IL	Panthers
Motlow College	Tullahoma, TN	Bucks
Mott Community College	Flint, MI	Bears
Mt. Hood Community College	Gresham, OR	Saints
Mt. San Antonio College	Walnut, CA	Mounties
Mt. San Jacinto College	San Jacinto, CA	Eagles
Mountain View College	Dallas, TX	Lions
Murray State College	Tishomingo, OK	Aggies
Muscatine Community College	Muscatine, IA	Indians
Muskegon Community College	Muskegon, MI	Jayhawks

N

Institution Name	Location	Nickname/Mascot
Napa Valley College	Napa, CA	Storm
Nassau Community College–SUNY	Garden City, NY	Lions
National Business College	Roanoke, VA	Eagles
Naugatuck Valley Community College	Waterbury, CT	Wave, The
Navarro College	Corsicana, TX	Bulldogs
Neosho County Community College	Chanute, KS	Panthers
Nebraska College of Tech Agriculture	Curtis, NE	Aggies
New Hampshire Com. Technical College	Laconia, NH	Centurions
New Hampshire Technical Institute	Concord, NH	Capitols
New Mexico Junior College	Hobbs, NM	Thunderbirds
New Mexico Military Institute	Roswell, NM	Broncos
New York City Technical College	Brooklyn, NY	Bees
Niagara County Com. College–SUNY	Sanborn, NY	Trailblazers
Normandale Community College	Bloomington, MN	Lions
North Arkansas College	Harrison, AR	Pioneers
North Central Missouri College	Trenton, MO	Pirates
North Central Technical Institute	Wausau, WI	Bears
North Central Texas College	Gainesville, TX	Lions
North Country Community College–SUNY	Saranac Lake, NY	Saints
North Dakota State College of Science	Wahpeton, ND	Wildcats
North Florida Community College	Madison, FL	Sentinels
North Hennepin Community College	Minneapolis, MN	Norsemen
North Idaho College	Coeur d'Alene, ID	Cardinals
North Iowa Area Community College	Mason City, IA	Trojans
North Lake College	Irving, TX	Blazers
North Shore Community College	Danvers, MA	Sea Hawks

Junior and Community Colleges—United States
Alphabetic Listing by Institution

Institution Name	Location	Nickname/Mascot
Northampton Community College	Bethlehem, PA	Spartans
Northeast Community College	Norfolk, NE	Hawks
Northeast Mississippi Community College	Booneville, MS	Tigers
Northeast Texas Community College	Mt. Pleasant, TX	Eagles
Northeastern Junior College	Sterling, CO	Plainsmen
Northeastern Oklahoma A&M	Miami, OK	Golden Norsemen
Northern Essex Community College	Haverhill, MA	Knights
Northern Maine Technical College	Presque Isle, ME	Falcons
Northern Oklahoma College	Tonkawa, OK	Mavericks
Northern Oklahoma College—Enid	Enid, OK	Jets
Northland Community & Tech College	Thief River Falls, MN	Pioneers
Northland Pioneer Community College	Holbrook, AZ	Golden Eagles
Northwest—Shoals Community College	Muscle Shoals, AL	Patriots
Northwest Alabama State Junior College	Phil Campbell, AL	Vikings
Northwest College	Powell, WY	Trappers
Northwest Mississippi Community College	Senatobia, MS	Rangers
Northwestern Connecticut Com. College	Winstead, CT	Pioneers
Norwalk Community College	Norwalk, CT	Panthers

O

Institution Name	Location	Nickname/Mascot
Oakland Community College	Waterford, MI	Raiders
Oakton Community College	Des Plaines, IL	Raiders
Ocean County College	Toms River, NJ	Vikings
Odessa College	Odessa, TX	Wranglers
Ohio State University—Lima Tech	Lima, OH	Barons
Ohio University—Lancaster	Lancaster, OH	Cougars
Ohio University—Zanesville	Zanesville, OH	Tracers
Ohlone College	Fremont, CA	Renegades
Okaloosa—Walton Community College	Niceville, FL	Raiders
Olive Harvey College—City College of Chicago	Chicago, IL	Panthers
Olney Central College	Olney, IL	Blue Knights
Olympic College	Bremerton, WA	Rangers
Onondaga Community College—SUNY	Syracuse, NY	Lazers
Orange Coast College	Costa Mesa, CA	Pirates
Orange County Community College—SUNY	Middletown, NY	Colts
Otero Junior College	La Junta, CO	Rattlers
Owens Community College	Toledo, OH	Express
Oxford College of Emory University	Oxford, GA	Eagles
Oxnard College	Oxnard, CA	Condors

Junior and Community Colleges—United States
Alphabetic Listing by Institution

Institution Name	Location	Nickname/Mascot
P		
Palm Beach Community College	Lake Worth, FL	Panthers
Palo Alto College	San Antonio, TX	Palominos
Palomar College	San Marcos, CA	Comets
Panola College	Carthage, TX	Ponies/Fillies
Paradise Valley Community College	Phoenix, AZ	Pumas
Paris Junior College	Paris, TX	Dragons
Parkland College	Champaign, IL	Cobras
Pasadena City College	Pasadena, CA	Lancers
Pasco-Hernando Community College	New Port Richey, FL	Conquistadors
Passaic County Community College	Paterson, NJ	Panthers
Paul Smith's College	Paul Smiths, NY	Bobcats
Pearl River Community College	Poplarville, MS	Wildcats
Peninsula Community College	Port Angeles, WA	Pirates
Pennsylvania College of Technology	Williamsport, PA	Wildcats
Penn State University—Altoona	Altoona, PA	Lions
Penn State University—Erie, Behrend Col.	Erie, PA	Behrend Lions
Penn Valley Community College	Kansas City, MO	Scouts
Pensacola Junior College	Pensacola, FL	Pirates
Philadelphia Community College	Philadelphia, PA	Colonials
Phillips County Community College	Helena, AR	Ridgerunners
Phoenix College	Phoenix, AZ	Bears
Pierce College	Lakewood, WA	Raiders
Pima Community College—East Campus	Tucson, AZ	Storm
Pima Community College—West Campus	Tucson, AZ	Aztecs
Pitt Community College	Greenville, NC	Bulldogs
Polk Community College	Winter Haven, FL	Vikings
Portland Community College	Portland, OR	Panthers
Porterville College	Porterville, CA	Pirates
Potomac State College of WVU	Keyser, WV	Catamounts
Prairie State College	Chicago Heights, IL	Pioneers
Pratt Community College	Pratt, KS	Beavers
Prince George's Community College	Largo, MD	Owls
Q		
Queensborough Com. College—CUNY	Bayside, NY	Tigers
Quincy College	Quincy, MA	Collegians
Quinsigamond Community College	Worcester, MA	Chiefs

Junior and Community Colleges—United States
Alphabetic Listing by Institution

Institution Name	Location	Nickname/Mascot
R		
Rainy River Community College	Internat'l Falls, MN	Voyageurs
Ranger College	Ranger, TX	Rangers
Raritan Valley Community College	North Branch, NJ	Golden Lions
Redlands Community College	El Reno, OK	Cougars
Redwoods, College of the	Eureka, CA	Corsairs
Reedley College	Reedley, CA	Tigers
Rend Lake College	Ina, IL	Warriors
Rhode Island, Community College of	Warwick, RI	Knights
Richland College	Dallas, TX	Thunderducks
Ricks College	Rexburg, ID	Vikings
Ridgewater College	Willmar, MN	Warriors
Rio Hondo College	Whittier, CA	Roadrunners
Riverland Community College	Austin, MN	Blue Devils
Riverside Community College	Riverside, CA	Tigers
Roane State Community College	Harriman, TN	Raiders
Rochester Community & Technical College	Rochester, MN	Yellowjackets
Rock Valley College	Rockford, IL	Golden Eagles
Rockingham Community College	Wentworth, NC	Eagles
Rockland Community College–SUNY	Suffern, NY	Hawks
Rose State College	Midwest City, OK	Raiders
Roxbury Community College	Roxbury Crossing, MA	Tigers
S		
Sacramento City College	Sacramento, CA	Panthers
Saddleback Community College	Mission Viejo, CA	Gauchos
Sage Junior College of Albany	Albany, NY	Sabres
Salem Community College	Carney's Point, NJ	Oaks
Salt Lake Community College	Salt Lake City, UT	Bruins
San Bernadino Valley College	San Bernadino, CA	Wolverines
San Diego City College	San Diego, CA	Knights
San Diego Mesa College	San Diego, CA	Olympians
San Francisco, City College of	San Francisco, CA	Rams
San Jacinto College–Central	Pasadena, TX	Ravens
San Jacinto College–North	Houston, TX	Gators
San Jacinto College–South	Houston, TX	Coyotes
San Joachin Delta College	Stockton, CA	Mustangs
San Jose City College	San Jose, CA	Jaguars
San Mateo, College of	San Mateo, CA	Bulldogs
Santa Ana College	Santa Ana, CA	Dons

Junior and Community Colleges—United States
Alphabetic Listing by Institution

Institution Name	Location	Nickname/Mascot
Santa Barbara City College	Santa Barbara, CA	Vaqueros
Santa Fe Community College	Gainesville, FL	Saints
Santa Monica College	Santa Monica, CA	Corsairs
Santa Rosa Junior College	Santa Rosa, CA	Bear Cubs
Sauk Valley Community College	Dixon, IL	Skyhawks
Schenectady County Community College	Schenectady, NY	Royals
Schoolcraft College	Livonia, MI	Ocelots
Scottsdale Community College	Scottsdale, AZ	Artichokes
Seattle Community College District	Seattle, WA	Storm
Selma University	Selma, AL	Bulldogs
Seminole Community College	Sanford, FL	Raiders
Seminole State College	Seminole, OK	Trojans/Belles
Sequoias, College of the	Visalia, CA	Giants
Seward County Community College	Liberal, KS	Saints
Shasta College	Redding, CA	Knights
Shawnee Community College	Ullin, IL	Saints
Shelton State Community College	Tuscaloosa, AL	Buccaneers
Sheridan College	Sheridan, WY	Generals
Shoreline Community College	Seattle, WA	Dolphins
Shorter College	N. Little Rock, AR	Bulldogs
Sierra College	Rocklin, CA	Wolverines
Sinclair Community College	Dayton, OH	Tartans
Siskiyous, College of the	Weed, CA	Eagles
Skagit Valley College	Mt. Vernon, WA	Cardinals
Skyline College	San Bruno, CA	Trojans
Snead State Community College	Boaz, AL	Parsons
Snow College	Ephraim, UT	Badgers
Solano Community College	Suisun City, CA	Falcons
South Carolina–Lancaster, University of	Lancaster, SC	Lancers
South Carolina–Salkehatch, University of	Allendale, SC	Indians
South Florida Community College	Avon Park, FL	Panthers
South Georgia College	Douglas, GA	Tigers
South Georgia Technical College	Americus, GA	Jets
South Mountain Community College	Phoenix, AZ	Cougars
South Plains College	Levelland, TX	Texans
South Puget Sound Community College	Olympia, WA	Clippers
South Suburban College	South Holland, IL	Bulldogs
Southeast Community College	Beatrice, NE	Storm
Southeastern Community College	Keokuk, IA	Komets
Southeastern Community College	West Burlington, IA	Blackhawks
Southeastern Community College	Whiteville, NC	Rams

Junior and Community Colleges—United States
Alphabetic Listing by Institution

Institution Name	Location	Nickname/Mascot
Southeastern Illinois College	Harrisburg, IL	Falcons
Southern Idaho, College of	Twin Falls, ID	Golden Eagles
Southern Maine Technical College	Portland, ME	Fighting Techs
Southern Maryland, College of	LaPlata, MD	Hawks
Southern Nevada, Community College of	North Las Vegas, NV	Coyotes
Southern State Community College	Hillsboro, OH	Patriots
Southern Union State Com. College	Wadley, AL	Bison
Southern University—Shreveport	Shreveport, LA	Jaguars
Southwest Mississippi Com. College	Summit, MS	Bears
S.W. Missouri State University—W. Plains	West Plains, MO	Grizzlies
Southwest Tennessee Community College	Memphis, TN	Saluqis
Southwest Texas Junior College	Uvalde, TX	Cowboys
Southwest Wisconsin Tech	Fennimore, WI	Chargers
Southwestern Community College	Creston, IA	Spartans
Southwestern Christian College	Terrell, TX	Rams
Southwestern College	Chula Vista, CA	Jaguars
Southwestern Illinois College	Belleville, IL	Blue Storm
Southwestern Indian Polytechnic Institute	Albuquerque, NM	Eagles
Southwestern Oregon Community College	Coos Bay, OR	Lakers
Spartanburg Methodist College	Spartanburg, SC	Pioneers
Spokane, Community Colleges of	Spokane, WA	Sasquatch
Spoon River College	Canton, IL	Crusaders
Springfield College—Illinois	Springfield, IL	Bulldogs
Springfield Technical Community College	Springfield, MA	Rams
St. Catherine College	St. Catherine, KY	Patriots
St. Charles Community College	St. Peters, MO	Cougars
St. Clair County Community College	Port Huron, MI	Skippers
St. John's River Community College	Palatka, FL	Vikings
St. Louis Com. College—Florissant Valley	St. Louis, MO	Norsemen
St. Louis Community College—Forest Park	St. Louis, MO	Highlanders
St. Louis Community College—Meramec	St. Louis, MO	Magic
St. Petersburg College	St. Petersburg, FL	Titans
State Fair Community College	Sedalia, MO	Roadrunners
Suffolk County Com. Col.—Selden (SUNY)	Selden, NY	Clippers
Suffolk County Com. Col.—Western (SUNY)	Brentwood, NY	Longhorns
Sullivan College	Louisville, KY	Executives
Sullivan County Community College—SUNY	Loch Sheldrake, NY	Generals
Suomi Junior College	Hancock, MI	Lions
Surry Community College	Dobson, NC	Knights
Sussex County Community College	Newton, NJ	Skylanders

Junior and Community Colleges—United States
Alphabetic Listing by Institution

Institution Name	Location	Nickname/Mascot

T

Institution Name	Location	Nickname/Mascot
Tacoma Community College	Tacoma, WA	Titans
Taft College	Taft, CA	Cougars
Tallahassee Community College	Tallahassee, FL	Eagles
Technical Career Institutes	New York, NY	Generals
Temple College	Temple, TX	Leopards
Terra Community College	Fremont, OH	Thunder
Texarkana College	Texarkana, TX	Bulldogs
Thaddeus Stevens College of Technology	Lancaster, PA	Bulldogs
Three Rivers Community College	Norwich, CT	Sonics
Three Rivers Community College	Poplar Bluff, MO	Raiders
Tompkins Cortland Com. College—SUNY	Dryden, NY	Panthers
Treasure Valley Community College	Ontario, OR	Chukars
Trinidad State Junior College	Trinidad, CO	Trojans
Trinity Valley Community College	Athens, TX	Cardinals
Triton College	River Grove, IL	Trojans
Truett-McConnell College	Cleveland, GA	Danes
Tunxis Community College	Farmington, CT	Tomahawks
Tyler Junior College	Tyler, TX	Apaches

U

Institution Name	Location	Nickname/Mascot
Ulster Community College—SUNY	Stone Ridge, NY	Senators
Umpqua Community College	Roseberg, OR	Timbermen
Union County College	Cranford, NJ	Owls
United Tribes Technical College	Bismarck, ND	Thunderbirds
Unity College	Unity, ME	Rams
Utah Valley State v College	West Orem, UT	Wolverines

V

Institution Name	Location	Nickname/Mascot
Valencia Community College	Orlando, FL	Matadors
Valley Forge Military College	Wayne, PA	Trojans
Ventura College	Ventura, CA	Pirates
Vermilion Community College	Ely, MN	Ironmen
Vermont Technical College	Randolph Center, VT	Green Knights
Vernon College	Vernon, TX	Chaparrals
Victor Valley Community College	Victorville, CA	Rams
Villa Maria College	Buffalo, NY	Vikings
Vincennes University	Vincennes, IN	Trailblazers
Volunteer State Community College	Gallatin, TN	Pioneers

Junior and Community Colleges—United States
Alphabetic Listing by Institution

Institution Name	Location	Nickname/Mascot
W		
Wabash Valley College	Mt. Carmel, IL	Warriors
Waldorf College	Forest City, IA	Warriors
Walla Walla Community College	Walla Walla, WA	Warriors
Wallace Community College—Dothan	Dothan, AL	Governors
Wallace Community College—Selma	Selma, AL	Patriots
Wallace State Com. College—Hanceville	Hanceville, AL	Lions
Walters State Community College	Morristown, TN	Senators
Waubonsee Community College	Sugar Grove, IL	Chiefs
Waukesha County Technical College	Pewaukee, WI	Owls
Wayne County Community College District	Detroit, MI	Wildcats
Weatherford College	Weatherford, TX	Coyotes
Wenatchee Valley Community College	Wenatchee, WA	Knights
Wentworth Military Academy & JC	Lexington, MO	Red Dragons
West Hills Community College	Coalinga, CA	Falcons
West Los Angeles College	Culver City, CA	Oilers
West Valley Community College	Saratoga, CA	Vikings
Westchester Community College—SUNY	Valhalla, NY	Vikings
Western Nebraska Community College	Scottsbluff, NE	Cougars
Western Oklahoma State College	Altus, OK	Pioneers
Western Texas College	Snyder, TX	Westerners
Western Wisconsin Technical College	La Crosse, WI	Cavaliers
Western Wyoming College	Rock Springs, WY	Spartans
Westmoreland County Community College	Youngwood, PA	Wolfpack
Wharton County Junior College	Wharton, TX	Pioneers
Whatcom Community College	Bellingham, WA	Orcas
Wilbur Wright College— City College of Chicago	Chicago, IL	Rams
Wilkes Community College	Wilkesboro, NC	Cougars
William Rainey Harper College	Palatine, IL	Hawks
Williamson Free School of MechnicalTrades	Media, PA	Mechanics
Williston State College	Williston, ND	Tetons
Wisconsin—Baraboo-Sauk, University of	Baraboo, WI	Barons
Wisconsin—Barron, University of	Rice Lake, WI	Chargers
Wisconsin—Fond du Lac, University of	Fond du Lac, WI	Centaurs
Wisconsin—Manitowoc, University of	Manitowoc, WI	Blue Devils
Wisconsin—Marathon, University of	Wausau, WI	Huskies
Wisconsin—Marinette, University of	Marinette, WI	Buccaneers
Wisconsin—Marshfield, University of	Marshfield, WI	Marauders
Wisconsin—Richland Center, University of	Richland Center, WI	Roadrunners

Junior and Community Colleges—United States
Alphabetic Listing by Institution

Institution Name	Location	Nickname/Mascot
Wisconsin—Rock County, University of	Janesville, WI	Rattlers
Wisconsin—Washington, University of	West Bend, WI	Wildcats
Wisconsin—Waukesha, University of	Waukesha, WI	Cougars
Wood Junior College	Mathiston, MS	Eagles
Wytheville Community College	Wytheville, VA	Gray Ghosts

Y

Institution Name	Location	Nickname/Mascot
Yakima Valley Community College	Yakima, WA	Yaks
Yavapai College	Prescott, AZ	Roughriders
Young Harris College	Young Harris, GA	Mountain Lions
Yuba Community College	Marysville, CA	49ers

Part 4

Junior and Community Colleges

United States

Alphabetic Listing by Nickname/Mascot

Did you know. . .

that it is hard to believe! The UC-Santa Cruz Banana Slugs. The banana slug is a slimy bright yellow (or banana) mollusk indigenous to the redwood forest surrounding the Santa Cruz campus. The students adopted the slug as a mascot back in the '60s as a ironic comment on the hyper-competitive world of college sports. The University actually tried to foist a new, less ridiculous nickname —Sea Lions—on the school in 1980, but the administration was shouted down by a student body whipped into a full frenzy over the debate.

Junior and Community Colleges—United States
Alphabetic Listing by Nickname/Mascot

Nickname/Mascot	Institution Name	Location

A

Nickname/Mascot	Institution Name	Location
****(Golf Only)	Augusta Technical College	Augusta, GA
49ers	Yuba College	Marysville, CA
Aggies	Murray State College	Tishomingo, OK
Aggies	Nebraska College of Technology Agriculture	Curtis, NE
Aliens	Lincoln School of Commerce	Lincoln, NE
Antelopes	Lamar Community College	Lamar, CO
Apaches	Cochise College	Douglas, AZ
Apaches	Tyler Junior College	Tyler, TX
Arabs	Imperial Valley College	Imperial, CA
Artichokes	Scottsdale Community College	Scottsdale, AZ
Atomics	Asheville–Buncombe Technical Junior College	Asheville, NC
Aztecs	Pima Community College–West Campus	Tucson, AZ
Badgers	Snow College	Ephraim, UT

B

Nickname/Mascot	Institution Name	Location
Barons	Burlington County College	Pemberton, NJ
Barons	Ohio State University–Lima	Lima, OH
Barons	Wisconsin–Baraboo-Sauk, University of	Baraboo, WI
Bear Cubs	Santa Rosa Junior College	Santa Rosa, CA
Bearcats	Lon Morris College	Jacksonville, TX
Bears	Bevill State Community College	Sumiton, AL
Bears	Bevill State Community College–Fayette	Fayette, AL
Bears	Brookhaven College	Farmers Branch, TX
Bears	Clinton Junior College	Rock Hill, SC
Bears	Des Moines Area Community College	Boone, IA
Bears	Harcum College (Women)	Bryn Mawr, PA
Bears	Mott Community College	Flint, MI
Bears	Phoenix College	Phoenix, AZ
Bears	Southwest Mississippi Community College	Summit, MS
Beavers	American River College	Sacramento, CA
Beavers	Champlain College	Burlington, VT
Beavers	Los Angeles Trade-Technical College	Los Angeles, CA
Beavers	Pratt Community College	Pratt, KS
Behrend Lions	Penn State University, Erie, Behrend College	Erie, PA
Bengals	Louisiana State University–Eunice	Eunice, LA
Bison	Southern Union State Community College	Wadley, AL
Blackhawks	Southeastern Community College	West Burlington, IA
Blazers	North Lake College	Irving, TX
Blue Devils	Hesser College	Manchester, NH

Junior and Community Colleges—United States
Alphabetic Listing by Nickname/Mascot

Nickname/Mascot	Institution Name	Location
Blue Devils	Kansas City Kansas Community College	Kansas City, KS
Blue Devils/Blue Angels	Kaskaskia College	Centralia, IL
Blue Devils	Merced College	Merced, CA
Blue Devils	Riverland Community College	Austin, MN
Blue Devils	Wisconsin—Manitowoc, University of	Manitowoc, WI
Blue Dragons	Hutchison Community College	Hutchison, KS
Blue Jays	Manor College	Jenkintown, PA
Blue Knights	Dakota County Technical College	Rosemount, MN
Blue Knights	Olney Central College	Olney, IL
Blue Storm	Southwestern Illinois College	Belleville, IL
Bluejays	Minnesota West Com. & Tech. Col.	Worthington, MN
Bobcats	Bryant & Stratton	Syracuse, NY
Bobcats	Central Oregon Community College	Bend, OR
Bobcats	Jones County Junior College	Ellisville, MS
Bobcats	Paul Smith's College	Paul Smith's, NY
Boll Weevils	Enterprise State Junior College	Enterprise, AL
Brahmas	Los Angeles Pierce College	Woodland Hills, CA
Braves	Black Hawk College—Moline	Moline, IL
Bridgers	Kent State University	East Liverpool, OH
Broncbusters	Garden City Community College	Garden City, KS
Broncos	Bronx Community College—CUNY	Bronx, NY
Broncos	New Mexico Military Institute	Roswell, NM
Broncos	Delhi College of Technology—SUNY	Delhi, NY
Bruins	Kellogg Community College	Battle Creek, MI
Bruins	Salt Lake Community College	Salt Lake City, UT
Buccaneers	Atlantic Cape Community College	Mays Landing, NJ
Buccaneers	Blinn College	Brenham, TX
Buccaneers	Catawba Valley Community College	Hickory, NC
Buccaneers	Dawson Community College	Glendive, MT
Buccaneers	Edison Community College	Fort Myers, FL
Buccaneers	Massachusetts Bay Community College	Wellesley Hills,MA
Buccaneers	Shelton State Community College	Tuscaloosa, AL
Buccaneers	Wisconsin—Marinette, University of	Marinette, WI
Bucks	Motlow College	Tullahoma, TN
Bulldogs	Allan Hancock College	Santa Maria, CA
Bulldogs	Bergen Community College	Paramus, NJ
Bulldogs	Bunker Hill Community College	Charlestown, MA
Bulldogs	Clarendon College	Clarendon, TX
Bulldogs	Dean College	Franklin, MA
Bulldogs	Georgia Military College	Milledgeville, GA
Bulldogs	Holmes Community College	Goodman, MS
Bulldogs	Mississippi Gulf Coast Community College	Perkinston, MS

Junior and Community Colleges—United States
Alphabetic Listing by Nickname/Mascot

Nickname/Mascot	Institution Name	Location
Bulldogs	Navarro College	Corsicana, TX
Bulldogs	Pitt Community College	Greenville, NC
Bulldogs	San Mateo, College of	San Mateo, CA
Bulldogs	South Suburban College	South Holland, IL
Bulldogs	Springfield College	Springfield, IL
Bulldogs	Texarkana College	Texarkana, TX
Bulldogs	Thaddeus Stevens College of Technology	Lancaster, PA

C

Cannoneers	Jefferson Community College–SUNY	Watertown, NY
Capitals	New Hampshire Technical Institute	Concord, NH
Cardinals	Baltimore County–Catonsville, Community College of	Catonsville, MD
Cardinals	Gadsden State Community College	Gadsden, AL
Cardinals	Hibbing Community College	Hibbing, MN
Cardinals	Labette Community College	Parsons, KS
Cardinals	Mineral Area College	Park Hills, MO
Cardinals	North Idaho College	Coeur d'Alene, ID
Cardinals	Skagit Valley College	Mt. Vernon, WA
Cardinals	Trinity Valley Community College	Athens, TX
Catamounts	Potomac State College of WVU	Keyser, WV
Cavaliers	Aquinas Junior College	Nashville, TN
Cavaliers	Bossier Parish Community College	Bossier City, LA
Cavaliers	Darton College	Albany, GA
Cavaliers	Davidson County Community College	Lexington, NC
Cavaliers	Johnson County Community College	Overland Park, KS
Cavaliers	Kankakee Community College	Kankakee, IL
Cavaliers	Western Wisconsin Technical College	La Crosse, WI
Centaurs	Maple Woods Community College	Kansas City, MO
Centurions	Bucks County Community College	Newtown, PA
Centurions	New Hampshire Com. Technical College	Laconia, NH
Challengers	Cuyahoga Community College	Highland Hills, OH
Chaparrals	DuPage, College of	Glen Ellyn, IL
Chaparrals	Midland College	Midland, TX
Chaparrals	Vernon College	Vernon, TX
Chargers	Ancilla College	Donaldson, IN
Chargers	Carl Sandburg College	Galesburg, IL
Chargers	Columbia State Community College	Columbia, TN
Chargers	Cypress College	Cypress, CA
Chargers	Edison Community College	Piqua, OH

Junior and Community Colleges—United States
Alphabetic Listing by Nickname/Mascot

Nickname/Mascot	Institution Name	Location
Chargers	Southwest Wisconsin Technical College	Fennimore, WI
Chargers	Wisconsin–Barron, University of	Rice Lake, WI
Chiefs	Quinsigamond Community College	Worcester, MA
Chiefs	Waubonsee Community College	Sugar Grove, IL
Chokers	Grays Harbor College	Aberdeen, WA
Chukars	Treasure Valley Community College	Ontario, OR
Claim Jumpers	Columbia College	Columbia, CA
Clippers	South Puget Sound Community College	Olympia, WA
Clippers	Suffolk County Com. College– Selden (SUNY)	Selden, NY
Cobras	Caldwell Community College & Tech. Inst.	Hudson, NC
Cobras	Parkland College	Champaign, IL
Collegians	Quincy College	Quincy, MA
Colonials	Philadelphia, Community College of	Philadelphia, PA
Colts	Canada College	Redwood City, CA
Colts	Middlesex County College	Edison, NJ
Colts	Orange County Community College–SUNY	Middletown, NY
Comets	Contra Costa College	San Pablo, CA
Comets	Cottey College (Women)	Nevada, MO
Comets	Palomar College	San Marcos, CA
Commodores	Capital Community College	Hartford, CT
Commodores	Gulf Coast Community College	Panama City, FL
Condors	Oxnard College	Oxnard, CA
Conquistadors	Dodge City Community College	Dodge City, KS
Conquistadors	Pasco-Hernando Community College	New Port Richey, FL
Corsairs	Redwoods, College of the	Eureka, CA
Corsairs	Santa Monica College	Santa Monica, CA
Cougars	Alameda, College of	Alameda, CA
Cougars	Allegheny County–Allegheny, Com. Col. of	Pittsburgh, PA
Cougars	Barton County Community College	Great Bend, KS
Cougars	Camden County College	Blackwood, NJ
Cougars	Canyons, College of the	Valencia, CA
Cougars	Central Carolina Community College	Sanford, NC
Cougars	Clackamas Community College	Oregon City, OR
Cougars	Cleveland State Community College	Cleveland, TN
Cougars	Clinton Community College–SUNY	Plattsburgh, NY
Cougars	Coastal Carolina Community College	Jacksonville, NC
Cougars	Columbus State Community College	Columbus, OH
Cougars	Cuesta College	San Luis Obispo, CA
Cougars	Frederick Community College	Frederick, MD
Cougars	Genesee Community College–SUNY	Batavia, NY

Junior and Community Colleges—United States
Alphabetic Listing by Nickname/Mascot

Nickname/Mascot	Institution Name	Location
Cougars	Highland Community College	Freeport, IL
Cougars	Holyoke Community College	Holyoke, MA
Cougars	Illinois Central College	East Peoria, IL
Cougars	Kalamazoo Valley Community College	Kalamazoo, MI
Cougars	Kent State University—Salem	Salem, OH
Cougars	Lassen Community College	Susanville, CA
Cougars	Lawson State Community College	Birmingham, AL
Cougars	Lehigh Carbon Community College	Schnecksville, PA
Cougars	Los Angeles Southwest College	Los Angeles, CA
Cougars	Manchester Community College	Manchester, CT
Cougars	Mid-State Technical College	Wisconsin Rapids, WI
Cougars	Ohio University—Lancaster	Lancaster, OH
Cougars	Redlands Community College	El Reno, OK
Cougars	South Mountain Community College	Phoenix, AZ
Cougars	St. Charles Community College	St. Peters, MO
Cougars	Taft College	Taft, CA
Cougars	Western Nebraska Community College	Scottsbluff, NE
Cougars	Wilkes Community College	Wilkesboro, NC
Cougars	Wisconsin—Waukesha, University of	Waukesha, WI
Cowboys	Connors State College	Warner, OK
Cowboys	Southwest Texas Junior College	Uvalde, TX
Coyotes	Cerro Coso Community College	Ridgecrest, CA
Coyotes	Chandler—Gilbert Community College	Chandler, AZ
Coyotes	Cuyamaca College	El Cajon, CA
Coyotes	San Jacinto College—South	Houston, TX
Coyotes	Southern Nevada, Community College of	N. Las Vegas, NV
Coyotes	Weatherford College	Weatherford, TX
Crusaders	Spoon River College	Canton, IL
Cyclones	Moraine Valley Community College	Palos Hills, IL
Cubs	Los Angeles City College	Los Angeles, CA

D

Danes	Truett-McConnell College	Cleveland, GA
Dolphins	Alvin Community College	Alvin, TX
Dolphins	Brunswick Community College	Supply, NC
Dolphins	Delgado Community College	New Orleans, LA
Dolphins	Shoreline Community College	Seattle, WA
Dons	De Anza College	Cupertino, CA
Dons	Santa Ana College	Santa Ana, CA
Dragons	Howard Community College	Columbia, MD
Dragons	Paris Junior College	Paris, TX
Dukes	Cumberland County College	Vineland, NJ

111

Junior and Community Colleges—United States
Alphabetic Listing by Nickname/Mascot

Nickname/Mascot	Institution Name	Location

E

Eagles	Alabama Southern Community College	Monroeville, AL
Eagles	Clark State Community College	Springfield, OH
Eagles	Dyersburg State Community College	Dyersburg, TN
Eagles	Flathead Valley Community College	Kalispell, MT
Eagles	Hinds Community College	Raymond, MS
Eagles	Illinois Valley Community College	Oglesby, IL
Eagles	Kirkwood Community College	Cedar Rapids, IA
Eagles	Laney College	Oakland, CA
Eagles	Linn State Technical College	Linn, MO
Eagles	Mary Holmes College	West Point, MS
Eagles	Mendocino College	Ukiah, CA
Eagles	Meridian Community College	Meridian, MS
Eagles	Mt. San Jacinto College	San Jacinto, CA
Eagles	National Business College	Roanoke, VA
Eagles	Northeast Texas Community College	Mt. Pleasant, TX
Eagles	Oxford College of Emory University	Oxford, GA
Eagles	Rockingham Community College	Wentworth, NC
Eagles	Siskiyous, College of the	Weed, CA
Eagles	Southwestern Indian Polytechnic Institute	Albuquerque, NM
Eagles	Tallahassee Community College	Tallahassee, FL
Express	Collin County Community College	Plano, TX
Express	Owens Community College	Toledo, OH

F

Falcons	Berkshire Community College	Pittsfield, MA
Falcons	Cerritos College	Norwalk, CA
Falcons	Daytona Beach Community College	Daytona Beach, FL
Falcons	Dutchess Community College– SUNY	Poughkeepsie, NY
Falcons	Florida College	Temple Terrace, FL
Falcons	Indian Hills Community College—Centerville	Centerville, IA
Falcons	Lackawanna College	Scranton, PA
Falcons	Montgomery College—Takoma Park	Takoma Park, MD
Falcons	Northern Maine Technical College	Presque Isle, ME
Falcons	Solano Community College	Suisun City, CA
Falcons	Southeastern Illinois College	Harrisburg, IL
Falcons	West Hills Community College	Coalinga, CA
Falcons	Wisconsin—Fond du Lac, University of	Fond du Lac, WI
Fighting Owls	Harford Community College	Bel Air, MD
Fighting Scots	McHenry County College	Crystal Lake, IL

Junior and Community Colleges—United States
Alphabetic Listing by Nickname/Mascot

Nickname/Mascot	Institution Name	Location
Fighting Techs	Southern Maine Technical College	Portland, ME
Fighting Tigers	Andrew College	Cuthbert, GA
Fighting Tigers	Cobleskill College of Ag. & Tech.–SUNY	Cobleskill, NY
Firebirds	Kirtland Community College	Roscommon, MI
Flames	Atlanta Area Technical College	Atlanta, GA
Flying Horsemen	Middlesex Community College	Middletown, CT
Free Spirit	Los Angeles Mission College	Sylmar, CA

G

Nickname/Mascot	Institution Name	Location
Gators	Green River Community College	Auburn, WA
Gators	San Jacinto College–North	Houston, TX
Gauchos	Glendale Community College	Glendale, AZ
Gauchos	Saddleback Community College	Mission Viejo, CA
Geckos	GateWay Community College	Phoenix, AZ
Generals	Hazard Community College	Jackson, KY
Generals	Herkimer County Community College	Herkimer, NY
Generals	Jackson State Community College	Jackson, TN
Generals	Sheridan College	Sheridan, WY
Generals	Sullivan County Community College–SUNY	Loch Sheldrake, NY
Generals	Technical Career Institutes	New York, NY
Giants	Sequoias, College of the	Visalia, CA
Giants	Keystone College	LaPlume, PA
Gilamonsters	Eastern Arizona College	Thatcher, AZ
Gladiators	Chabot College	Hayward, CA
Golden Eagles	Eastern Maine Technical College	Bangor, ME
Golden Eagles	Eastern Utah, College of	Price, UT
Golden Eagles	Feather River College	Quincy, CA
Golden Eagles	Laramie County Community College	Cheyenne, WY
Golden Eagles	Northland Pioneer Community College	Holbrook, AZ
Golden Eagles	Rock Valley College	Rockford, IL
Golden Eagles	Southern Idaho, College of	Twin Falls, ID
Golden Lions	Raritan Valley Community College	North Branch, NJ
Golden Norsemen	Northeastern Oklahoma A&M	Miami, OK
Golden Rams	Anoka–Ramsey Community College	Coon Rapids, MN
Golden Stallions/Golden Fillies	Abraham Baldwin Agricultural College	Tifton, GA
Governors	Wallace Community College–Dothan	Dothan, AL
Green Knights	Vermont Technical College	Randolph Center, VT
Greyhounds	Fort Scott Community College	Fort Scott, KS
Greyhounds	Moberly Area Community College	Moberly, MO
Griffins	Grossmont College	El Cajon, CA
Grizzlies	Butler County Community College	El Dorado, KS

113

Junior and Community Colleges—United States
Alphabetic Listing by Nickname/Mascot

Nickname/Mascot	Institution Name	Location
Grizzlies	S.W. Missouri State University—West Plains	West Plains, MO
Gryphons	Montgomery College—Germantown	Germantown, MD

H

Harriers	Miami—Hamilton, University of	Hamilton, OH
Harvesters	Eastfield College	Mesquite, TX
Hawks	Columbia Basin College	Pasco, WA
Hawks	Cosumnes River College	Sacramento, CA
Hawks	Hagerstown Community College	Hagerstown, MD
Hawks	Harper College	Palatine, IL
Hawks	Harrisburg Area Community College	Harrisburg, PA
Hawks	Henry Ford Community College	Dearborn, MI
Hawks	Hillsborough Community College	Tampa, FL
Hawks	Housatonic Community College	Bridgeport, CT
Hawks	Howard College	Big Spring, TX
Hawks	Las Positas College	Livermore, CA
Hawks	Malcolm X College—City College of Chicago	Chicago, IL
Hawks	Mohawk Valley Community College	Utica, NY
Hawks	Northeast Community College	Norfolk, NE
Hawks	Rockland Community College— SUNY	Suffern, NY
Hawks	Santiago Canyon College	Orange, CA
Hawks	Southern Maryland, College of	LaPlata, MD
Hawks	William Rainey Harper College	Palatine, IL
Helmsmen	Bellevue Community College	Bellevue, WA
Highlanders	Gordon College	Barnesville, GA
Highlanders/Highlassies	McLennan Community College	Waco, TX
Highlanders	St. Louis Community College—Forest Park	St. Louis, MO
Hilltoppers	Ohio University—Chillicothe	Chillicothe, OH
Hornets	Broome Community College—SUNY	Binghamton, NY
Hornets	Fullerton College	Fullerton, CA
Hurricanes	Louisburg College	Louisburg, NC
Huskers	Clinton Community College	Clinton, IA
Huskies	East Los Angeles College	Monterey Park, CA
Huskies	Wisconsin—Marathon, University of	Wausau, WI

I

Indians	Chipola Community College	Marianna, FL
Indians	Itawamba Community College	Fulton, MS
Indians	Lake Michigan College	Benton Harbor, MI

Junior and Community Colleges—United States
Alphabetic Listing by Nickname/Mascot

Nickname/Mascot	Institution Name	Location
Indians	Mid-Plains Community College Area–McCook	McCook, NE
Indians	Muscatine Community College	Muscatine, IA
Indians	South Carolina–Salkehatch, University of	Allendale, SC
Ironmen	Vermilion Community College	Ely, MN

J

Jaguars	Danville Area Community College	Danville, IL
Jaguars	Georgia Perimeter College	Dunwoody, GA
Jaguars	Jacksonville College	Jacksonville, TX
Jaguars	Jamestown Community College, Olean–SUNY	Olean, NY
Jaguars	Johnson College	Scranton, PA
Jaguars	San Jose City College	San Jose, CA
Jaguars	Southern University–Shreveport	Shreveport, LA
Jaguars	Southwestern College	Chula Vista, CA
Jayhawks	Jamestown Community College	Jamestown, NY
Jayhawks	Muskegon Community College	Muskegon, MI
Jersey Blues	Brookdale Community College	Lincroft, NJ
Jets	Miramar College	San Diego, CA
Jets	Northern Oklahoma College–Enid	Enid, OK
Jets	South Georgia Technical College	Americus, GA

K

Kats	Erie Community College–SUNY	Buffalo, NY
Knights	Aiken Technical College	Aiken, SC
Knights	Baltimore County–Essex, Com. Col. of	Baltimore, MD
Knights	Edward Williams College	Hackensack, NJ
Knights	Essex Community College	Baltimore, MD
Knights	Globe Institute of Technology	New York, NY
Knights	Mid-Plains Com. College Area–North Platte	North Platte, NE
Knights	Montgomery College–Rockville	Rockville, MD
Knights	Northern Essex Community College	Haverhill, MA
Knights	Rhode Island, Community College of	Warwick, RI
Knights	San Diego City College	San Diego, CA
Knights	Shasta College	Redding, CA
Knights	Surry Community College	Dobson, NC
Knights	Wenatchee Valley Community College	Wenatchee, WA
Kougars	Kishwaukee College	Malta, IL

Junior and Community Colleges—United States
Alphabetic Listing by Nickname/Mascot

Nickname/Mascot	Institution Name	Location

L

Lakers	Finger Lakes Community College	Canadaigua, NY
Lakers	Garrett Community College	McHenry, MD
Lakers	Iowa Lakes Community College	Estherville, IA
Lakers	Lake Land College	Mattoon, IL
Lakers	Lake–Sumter Community College	Leesburg, FL
Lakers	Lakeland Community College	Kirtland, OH
Lakers	Longview Community College	Lee's Summit, MO
Lakers	Southwestern Oregon Community College	Coos Bay, OR
Lakers	Wright State University–Lake Campus	Celina, OH
Lancers	Eastern Wyoming College	Torrington, WY
Lancers	Lake County, College of	Grayslake, IL
Lancers	Lenoir Community College	Kinston, NC
Lancers	Manatee Community College	Bradenton, FL
Lancers	Pasadena City College	Pasadena, CA
Lancers	South Carolina–Lancaster, University of	Lancaster, SC
Landsharks	Landmark College	Putney, VT
Larks	Hesston College	Hesston, KS
Lasers	Irvine Valley College	Irvine, CA
Lazers	Onondaga Community College–SUNY	Syracuse, NY
Leopards	Temple College	Temple, TX
Lions	Arkansas–Fort Smith, University of	Fort Smith, AK
Lions	Baltimore County–Dundalk, Com. Col. of	Baltimore, MD
Lions	Brown Mackie College, The	Salina, KS
Lions	East Mississippi Community College	Scooba, MS
Lions	Gateway Community College	New Haven, CT
Lions	Mountain View College	Dallas, TX
Lions	Nassau Community College–SUNY	Garden City, NY
Lions	North Central Texas College	Gainesville, TX
Lions	Penn State University–Altoona	Altoona, PA
Lions	Wallace State Community College–Hanceville	Hanceville, AL
Lobos	Monterey Peninsula College	Monterey, CA
Loggers	Lincoln Land Community College	Springfield, IL
Longhorns	Suffolk County Community College– West (SUNY)	Brentwood, NY
Lumberjacks	Alpena Community College	Alpena, MI
Lumberjacks	Minot State University– Bottineau	Bottineau, ND
Lynx	Lincoln College	Lincoln, IL

Junior and Community Colleges—United States
Alphabetic Listing by Nickname/Mascot

Nickname/Mascot	Institution Name	Location
M		
Magic	St. Louis Community College–Meramec	St. Louis, MO
Marauders	Antelope Valley College	Lancaster, CA
Marauders	Minneapolis Community & Tech. Col.	Minneapolis, MN
Marauders	Wisconsin–Marshfield, University of	Marshfield, WI
Mariners	Coastal Georgia Community College	Brunswick, GA
Mariners	Marin, College of	Kentfield, CA
Mariners	Marymount College	Rancho Palos Verde, CA
Matadors	Arizona Western College	Yuma, AZ
Matadors	Valencia Community College	Orlando, FL
Mavericks	Mitchell Community College	Statesville, NC
Mavericks	Northern Oklahoma College–Tonkawa	Tonkawa, OK
Mechanics	Williamson Free School & Mech. Trades	Media, PA
Monarchs	Los Angeles Valley College	Van Nuys, CA
Monarchs	Macomb Community College	Warren, MI
Mountain Lions	Young Harris College	Young Harris, GA
Mountaineers	Adirondack Community College–SUNY	Queensbury, NY
Mountaineers	Eastern Oklahoma State College	Wilburton, OK
Mounties	Mt. San Antonio College	Walnut, CA
Mustangs	Central Baptist College	Conway, AR
Mustangs	Central Maine Technical College	Auburn, ME
Mustangs	Los Medanos College	Pittsburg, CA
Mustangs	Monroe College	Bronx, NY
Mustangs	Morrisville College of Ag. & Tech.–SUNY	Morrisville, NY
Mustangs	San Joachin Delta College	Stockton, CA
Mystics	Bismarck State College	Bismarck, ND
N		
Norse	Mesabi Range Community & Technical College	Virginia, MN
Norsemen	North Hennepin Community College	Minneapolis, MN
Norsemen	St. Louis Community College–Florissant Valley	St. Louis, MO
Northstars	Canton College of Technology–SUNY	Canton, NY
O		
Oaks	Salem Community College	Carney's Point, NJ
Ocelots	Schoolcraft College	Livonia, MI
Oilers	West Los Angeles College	Culver City, CA

Junior and Community Colleges—United States
Alphabetic Listing by Nickname/Mascot

Nickname/Mascot	Institution Name	Location
Olympians	San Diego Mesa College	San Diego, CA
Orcas	Whatcom Community College	Bellingham, WA
Owls	Citrus College	Glendora, CA
Owls	Foothill College	Los Altos Hills,CA
Owls	Prince George's Community College	Largo, MD
Owls	Union County College	Cranford, NJ
Owls	Waukesha County Technical College	Pewaukee, WI

P

Nickname/Mascot	Institution Name	Location
Palominos	Laredo Community College	Laredo, TX
Palominos	Palo Alto College	San Antonio, TX
Panthers	Chaffey College	Rancho Cucamonga, CA
Panthers	Craven Community College	New Bern, NC
Panthers	Ellsworth Community College	Iowa Falls, IA
Panthers	Hartnell Community College	Salinas, CA
Panthers	Borough of Manhattan Com. Col.–CUNY	New York, NY
Panthers	Moraine Park Technical College	Fond du Lac, WI
Panthers	Morton College	Cicero, IL
Panthers	Neosho County Community College	Chanute, KS
Panthers	Norwalk Community College	Norwalk, CT
Panthers	Ohio University–Eastern	St. Clairsville, OH
Panthers	Olive-Harvey College (City College of Chicago)	Chicago, IL
Panthers	Palm Beach Community College	Lake Worth, FL
Panthers	Passaic County Community College	Paterson, NJ
Panthers	Portland Community College	Portland, OR
Panthers	Sacramento City College	Sacramento, CA
Panthers	South Florida Community College	Avon Park, FL
Panthers	Tompkins Cortland Community College–SUNY	Dryden, NY
Parsons	Snead State Community College	Boaz, AL
Patriots	Brandywine College	Wilmington, DE
Patriots	Central Florida Community College	Ocala, FL
Patriots	DeKalb College	Dunwoody, GA
Patriots	Northwest–Shoals Community College–Phil Campbell	Phil Campbell, AL
Patriots	Southern State Community College	Hillsboro, OH
Patriots	St. Catherine College	St. Catherine, KY
Patriots	Wallace Community College–Selma	Selma, AL
Penguins	Clark College	Vancouver, WA
Phantoms	Delaware County Community College	Media, PA

Junior and Community Colleges—United States
Alphabetic Listing by Nickname/Mascot

Nickname/Mascot	Institution Name	Location
Pioneers	Alfred State College of Technology—SUNY	Alfred, NY
Pioneers	Anne Arundel Community College	Arnold, MD
Pioneers	Butler County Community College	Butler, PA
Pioneers	Crowley's Ridge College	Paragould, AK
Pioneers	Delta College	University Center, MI
Pioneers	Indian River Community College	Ft. Pierce, FL
Pioneers	Indiana University—East	Richmond, IN
Pioneers	Jefferson State Community College	Birmingham, AL
Pioneers	Miles Community College	Miles City, MT
Pioneers	North Arkansas College	Harrison, AR
Pioneers	Northland Community & Technical College	Thief River Falls, MN
Pioneers	Northwestern Connecticut Community College	Winstead, CT
Pioneers	Prairie State College	Chicago Heights, IL
Pioneers	Spartanburg Methodist College	Spartanburg, SC
Pioneers	Volunteer State Community College	Gallatin, TN
Pioneers	Western Oklahoma State College	Altus, OK
Pioneers	Wharton County Junior College	Wharton, TX
Pirates	Chattahoochee Valley Community College	Phenix City, AL
Pirates	Independence Community College	Independence, KS
Pirates	Modesto Junior College	Modesto, CA
Pirates	North Central Missouri College	Trenton, MO
Pirates	Orange Coast College	Costa Mesa, CA
Pirates	Peninsula College	Port Angeles, WA
Pirates	Pensacola Junior College	Pensacola, FL
Pirates	Porterville College	Porterville, CA
Pirates	Ventura College	Ventura, CA
Plainsmen	Frank Phillips College	Borger, TX
Plainsmen	Northeastern Junior College	Sterling, CO
Pointers	Connecticut—Avery Point, University of	Groton, CT
Ponies/Fillies	Panola College	Carthage, TX
Prairie Dogs	Ohio State University—Marion	Marion, OH
Pumas	Paradise Valley Community College	Phoenix, AZ

R

Raiders	Blanton Junior College	Asheville, NC
Raiders	Central Community College—Platte	Columbus, NE
Raiders	Central Lakes College—Brainerd	Brainerd, MN
Raiders	Fulton—Montgomery Com. College (SUNY)	Johnstown, NY
Raiders	Grand Rapids Community College	Grand Rapids, MI
Raiders	Moorpark College	Moorpark, CA

Junior and Community Colleges—United States
Alphabetic Listing by Nickname/Mascot

Nickname/Mascot	Institution Name	Location
Raiders	Oakland Community College	Waterford, MI
Raiders	Oakton Community College	Des Plaines, IL
Raiders	Okaloosa–Walton Community College	Niceville, FL
Raiders	Pierce College	Lakewood, WA
Raiders	Roane State Community College	Harriman, TN
Raiders	Rose State College	Midwest City, OK
Raiders	Seminole Community College	Sanford, FL
Raiders	Three Rivers Community College	Poplar Bluff, MO
Rams	Fresno City College	Fresno, CA
Rams	Gavilan College	Gilroy, CA
Rams	San Francisco, City College of	San Francisco, CA
Rams	Southeastern Community College	Whiteville, NC
Rams	Southwestern Christian College	Terrell, TX
Rams	Springfield Technical Community College	Springfield, MA
Rams	Unity College	Unity, ME
Rams	Victor Valley Community College	Victorville, CA
Rams	Wilbur Wright College–City College of Chicago	Chicago, IL
Rangers	Kilgore College	Kilgore, TX
Rangers	Northwest Mississippi Community College	Senatobia, MS
Rangers	Olympic College	Bremerton, WA
Rangers	Ranger College	Ranger, TX
Rattlers	Otero Junior College	La Junta, CO
Rattlers	Wisconsin–Rock County, University of	Janesville, WI
Ravens	San Jacinto College–Central	Pasadena, TX
Rebels	Dixie State College of Utah	St. George, UT
Rebels	East Central College	Union, MO
Rebels	Hill College	Hillsboro, TX
Red Barons	Corning Community College–SUNY	Corning, NY
Red Devils	Allen County Community College	Iola, KS
Red Devils	Baltimore City Community College	Baltimore, MD
Red Devils	Lower Columbia College	Longview, WA
Red Dragons	Wentworth Military Academy & Junior College	Lexington, MO
Red Eyed Panthers	Atlanta Metropolitan College	Atlanta, GA
Red Ravens	Coffeyville Community College	Coffeyville, KS
Reivers	Iowa Western Community College	Council Bluffs, IA
Renegades	Bakersfield College	Bakersfield, CA
Renegades	Ohlone College	Fremont, CA
Ridgerunners	Phillips County Community College	Helena, AR
Roadrunners	Angelina College	Lufkin, TX
Roadrunners	Butte College	Oroville, CA
Roadrunners	Delaware Technical & Com. College (Owens)	Georgetown, DE
Roadrunners	Desert, College of the	Palm Desert, CA

Junior and Community Colleges—United States
Alphabetic Listing by Nickname/Mascot

Nickname/Mascot	Institution Name	Location
Roadrunners	Gloucester County College	Sewell, NJ
Roadrunners	Linn–Benton Community College	Albany, OR
Roadrunners	Rio Hondo College	Whittier, CA
Roadrunners	State Fair Community College	Sedalia, MO
Roadrunners	Wisconsin–Richland Center,University of	Richland Center, WI
Rockets	Reading Area Community College	Reading, PA
Roughriders	Crowder College	Neosho, MO
Roughriders	Yavapai College	Prescott, AZ
Royals	Lake Region State College	Devils Lake, ND
Royals	Schenectady County Community College	Schenectady, NY
Runnin' Rebels	Lee College	Baytown, TX
Rustlers	Central Wyoming College	Riverton, WY
Rustlers	Golden West College	Huntington Beach, CA

S

Sabres	Sage Junior College of Albany	Albany, NY
Saints	Allegheny County Boyce Community College of	Monroeville, PA
Saints	Lurleen B. Wallace Junior College	Andalusia, AL
Saints	Mercyhurst College—North East	North East, PA
Saints	Mission College	Santa Clara, CA
Saints	Mt. Hood Community College	Gresham, OR
Saints	North Country Community College–SUNY	Saranac Lake, NY
Saints	Santa Fe Community College	Gainesville, FL
Saints	Seward County Community College	Liberal, KS
Saints	Shawnee Community College	Ullin, IL
Saluqis	Southwest Tennessee Community College	Memphis, TN
Samsons	Gogebic Community College	Ironwood, MI
Sasquatch	Spokane Community College	Spokane, WA
Scotties	Highland Community College	Highland, KS
Scouts	Penn Valley Community College	Kansas City, MO
Screaming Eagles	Scott Community College	Bettendorf, IA
Sea Devils	Cape Fear Community College	Wilmington, NC
Sea Hawks	North Shore Community College	Danvers, MA
Seahawks	Briarcliffe College	Bethpage, NY
Seahawks	Broward Community College	Ft. Lauderdale, FL
Seahawks	Broward Community College–Central Campus	Davie, FL
Seahawks	Broward Community College–North Campus	Coconut Creek, FL
Seahawks	Cabrillo College	Aptos, CA
Seahawks	Cecil Community College	North East, MD
Seahawks	Los Angeles Harbor College	Wilmington, CA
Senators	Ulster Community College–SUNY	Stone Ridge, NY

Junior and Community Colleges—United States
Alphabetic Listing by Nickname/Mascot

Nickname/Mascot	Institution Name	Location
Senators	Walters State Community College	Morristown, TN
Sentinels	North Florida Community College	Madison, FL
Sharks	Miami-Dade Community College	Miami, FL
Silver Knights	Central Penn College	Summerdale, PA
Skeeters	Delaware Technical & Community College (Terry)	Dover, DE
Skipjacks	Chesapeake College	Wye Mills, MD
Skippers	St. Clair County Community College	Port Huron, MI
Skyhawks	Sauk Valley Community College	Dixon, IL
Skylanders	Sussex County Community College	Newton, NJ
Sonics	Three Rivers Community College	Norwich, CT
Spartans	Cayuga Community College—SUNY	Auburn, NY
Spartans	Colorado Northwestern Community College	Rangeley, CO
Spartans	Elgin Community College	Elgin, IL
Spartans	Fergus Falls Community College	Fergus Falls, MN
Spartans	James Sprunt Community College	Kenansville, NC
Spartans	MiraCosta College	Oceanside, CA
Spartans	Northampton Community College	Bethlehem, PA
Spartans	Southwestern Community College	Creston, IA
Spartans	Western Wyoming College	Rock Springs, WY
Spirit	Delaware Technical & Community College (Stanton-Wilmington)	Newark, DE
Stars	Florida Community College at Jacksonville	Jacksonville, FL
Stars	Lansing Community College	Lansing, MI
Statesmen	Kennedy-King College (City College of Chicago)	Chicago, IL
Statesmen	Lincoln Trail College	Robinson, IL
Storm	Chemeketa Community College	Salem, OR
Storm	Napa Valley College	Napa, CA
Storm	Pima Community College—East Campus	Tucson, AZ
Storm	Seattle Community College	Seattle, WA
Storm	Southeast Community College	Beatrice, NE
Stormers	Milwaukee Area Technical College	Milwaukee, WI
Sun Chiefs	Faulkner State Community College	Bay Minette, AL
Suns	Cedar Valley College	Lancaster, TX
Suns	Mississippi County Community College	Blytheville, AR
Surge	Cincinnati State Technical & Community College	Cincinnati, OH

T

Tartans	Sinclair Community College	Dayton, OH
Tartars	Compton Community College	Compton, CA
Tejanos	El Paso Community College	El Paso, TX

Junior and Community Colleges—United States
Alphabetic Listing by Nickname/Mascot

Nickname/Mascot	Institution Name	Location
Tetons	Williston State College	Williston, ND
Texans	South Plains College	Levelland, TX
Thunder	Terra Community College	Fremont, OH
Thunderbirds or T-Birds	Casper College	Casper, WY
Thunderbirds	Cloud County Community College	Concordia, KS
Thunderbirds	Highline Community College	Des Moines, WA
Thunderbirds	Merritt College	Oakland, CA
Thunderbirds	Mesa Community College	Mesa, AZ
Thunderbirds	New Mexico Junior College	Hobbs, NM
Thunderbirds	United Tribes Technical College	Bismarck, ND
Thunderducks	Richland College	Dallas, TX
ThunderHawks	Miami–Middletown, University of	Middletown, OH
Tigers	Allegheny County–South, Community College of	West Mifflin, PA
Tigers	Central Piedmont Community College	Charlotte, NC
Tigers	Chattanooga State Technical Community College	Chattanooga, TN
Tigers	Cincinnati Technical College	Cincinnati, OH
Tigers	Coahoma Junior College	Clarksdale, MS
Tigers	Cowley College	Arkansas City, KS
Tigers	Forsyth Technical Community College	Winston-Salem, NC
Tigers	Hiwassee College	Madisonville, TN
Tigers	Marion Military Institute	Marion, AL
Tigers	Marshalltown Community College	Marshalltown, IA
Tigers	Northeast Mississippi Community College	Booneville, MS
Tigers	Queensborough Community College–CUNY	Bayside, NY
Tigers	Reedley College	Reedley, CA
Tigers	Riverside Community College	Riverside, CA
Tigers	Roxbury Community College	Roxbury Crossing, MA
Tigers	South Georgia College	Douglas, GA
Timbermen	Umpqua Community College	Roseberg, OR
Timberwolves	Blue Mountain Community College	Pendleton, OR
Timberwolves	Lake City Community College	Lake City, FL
Titans	Beaver County, Community College of	Monaca, PA
Titans	Brevard Community College	Cocoa, FL
Titans	Lane Community College	Eugene, OR
Titans	Morris, County College of	Randolph, NJ
Titans	Ohio State University–Newark	Newark, OH
Titans	St. Petersburg College	St. Petersburg, FL
Titans	Tacoma Community College	Tacoma, WA
Tomahawks	Tunxis Community College	Farmington, CT
Tornadoes	Brevard College	Brevard, NC
Tracers	Ohio University–Zanesville	Zanesville, OH
Trail Blazers	John Wood Community College	Quincy, IL

Junior and Community Colleges—United States
Alphabetic Listing by Nickname/Mascot

Nickname/Mascot	Institution Name	Location
Trailblazers	Arkansas State University—Mountain Home	Mountain Home, AR
Trailblazers	Centralia College	Centralia, WA
Trailblazers	Lewis & Clark Community College	Godfrey, IL
Trailblazers	Luzerne County Community College	Nanticoke, PA
Trailblazers	Niagara County Community College—SUNY	Sanborn, NY
Trailblazers	Ohio University—Southern	Ironton, OH
Trailblazers	Vincennes University	Vincennes, IN
Trappers	Northwest College	Powell, WY
Tribunes	Monroe Community College—SUNY	Rochester, NY
Tritons	Edmonds Community College	Lynnwood, WA
Tritons	Iowa Central Community College	Fort Dodge, IA
Trojans	Allegheny College of Maryland	Cumberland, MD
Trojans	Central Alabama Community College	Alexander City, AL
Trojans	Colby Community College	Colby, KS
Trojans	Everett Community College	Everett, WA
Trojans	Mississippi Delta Community College	Moorhead, MS
Trojans	North Iowa Area Community College	Mason City, IA
Trojans/Belles	Seminole State College	Seminole, OK
Trojans	Skyline College	San Bruno, CA
Trojans	Trinidad State Junior College	Trinidad, CO
Trojans	Triton College Junior College	River Grove, IL
Trojans	Valley Forge Military College	Wayne, PA
Twins	Columbia—Greene Community College (SUNY)	Hudson, NY

V

Nickname/Mascot	Institution Name	Location
Vaqueros	Central Arizona College	Coolidge, AZ
Vaqueros	Glendale College	Glendale, CA
Vaqueros	Santa Barbara City College	Santa Barbara, CA
Vikings	Barstow College	Barstow, CA
Vikings	Bethany Lutheran College	Mankato, MN
Vikings	Big Bend Community College	Moses Lake, WA
Vikings	Carl Albert State College	Poteau, OH
Vikings	Diablo Valley College	Pleasant Hill, CA
Vikings	Glen Oaks Community College	Centreville, MI
Vikings	Grayson County College	Denison, TX
Vikings	Hudson Valley Community College— SUNY	Troy, NY
Vikings	Itasca Community College	Grand Rapids, MN
Vikings	Jefferson College	Hillsboro, MO
Vikings	Kent State University—Ashtabula	Ashtabula, OH
Vikings	Long Beach City College	Long Beach, CA

Junior and Community Colleges—United States
Alphabetic Listing by Nickname/Mascot

Nickname/Mascot	Institution Name	Location
Vikings	Mercer County Community College	Trenton, NJ
Vikings	Ocean County College	Toms River, NJ
Vikings	Polk Community College	Winter Haven, FL
Vikings	Ricks College	Rexburg, ID
Vikings	St. John's River Community College	Palatka, FL
Vikings	West Valley Community College	Saratoga, CA
Vikings	Westchester Community College—SUNY	Valhalla, NY
Volunteers	John A. Logan College	Carterville, IL
Voyageurs	Rainy River Community College	Internat'l Falls, MN

W

Warhawks	Jefferson Davis Community College	Brewton, AL
Warriors	Akron—Wayne College, University of	Orrville, OH
Warriors	Black Hawk College—East	Kewanee, IL
Warriors	Diné College	Tsaile, AZ
Warriors	Dull Knife Memorial College	Lame Deer, MT
Warriors	East Central Community College	Decatur, MS
Warriors	El Camino College	Torrance, CA
Warriors	Indian Hills Community College—Ottumwa	Ottumwa, IA
Warriors	Massasoit Community College	Brockton, MA
Warriors	Miami University—Middletown	Middletown, OH
Warriors	Middle Georgia College	Cochran, GA
Warriors	Rend Lake College	Ina, IL
Warriors	Ridgewater College	Willmar, MN
Warriors	St. Louis—Meramec Community College	St. Louis, MO
Warriors	Wabash Valley College	Mt. Carmel, IL
Warriors	Waldorf College	Forest City, IA
Warriors	Walla Walla Community College	Walla Walla, WA
Wave, The	Kingsborough Community College—CUNY	Brooklyn, NY
Wave, The	Naugatuck Valley Community College	Waterbury, CT
Westerners/Dusters	Western Texas College	Snyder, TX
Whitecaps	Galveston College	Galveston, TX
Wildcats	Bishop State Community College	Mobile, AL
Wildcats	Wayne County Community College District	Detroit, MI
Wildcats	Wisconsin—Washington, University of	West Bend, WI
Wildcats	North Dakota State College of Science	Wahpeton, ND
Wildcats	Pearl River Community College	Poplarville, MS
Wildcats	Pennsylvania College of Technology	Williamsport, PA
Wolfpack	Westmoreland County Community College	Youngwood, PA
WolfPack	Madison Area Technical College	Madison, WI

Junior and Community Colleges—United States
Alphabetic Listing by Nickname/Mascot

Nickname/Mascot	Institution Name	Location
Wolverines	Essex County College	Newark, NJ
Wolverines	San Bernadino Valley College	San Bernadino, CA
Wolverines	Sierra College	Rocklin, CA
Wolverines	Utah Valley State College	West Orem, UT
Wolves	Copiah–Lincoln Community College	Wesson, MS
Wolves	Joliet Junior College	Joliet, IL
Wranglers	Cisco Junior College	Cisco, TX
Wranglers	Odessa College	Odessa, TX

Y

Nickname/Mascot	Institution Name	Location
Yaks	Yakima Valley Community College	Yakima, WA
Yellowjackets	Kemper Military Junior College	Boonville, MO
Yellowjackets	Rochester Community & Technical College	Rochester, MN

Part 5

Junior, Senior, and Community Colleges

Canada

Alphabetic Listing by Institution

Did you know. . .

that the "Billikens" have been the mascot of Saint Louis University since 1910, when someone (there are various versions of the story) noted the school's football coach, Charlie "Moonface" Bender looked like a popular little carved doll of the era known as the Billiken?

For several years, the bullet-shaped imp was everywhere and in every form (belt buckles, salt and pepper shakers, pickle forks, hood ornaments) but the fad died out in 1912. Female Billikens are also called Millikens.

Junior, Senior, and Community Colleges—Canada
Alphabetic Listing by Institution

Institution Name	Location	Nickname/Mascot

A

Acadia University	Wolfville, NS	Axemen
Ahuntsic, Collège	Montréal, PQ	Indiens
Alberta, University of	Edmonton, ALTA	Golden Bears/Pandas
Aldersgate College	Moosejaw, SASK	Flames
Algoma University College	Sault St. Marie, ONT	Thunderbirds
Algonquin College	Nepean, ONT	Thunder
André–Grasset, Collège	Montréal, PQ	Phénix
André-Laurendeau, Collège	Lasalle, PQ	Ideal
Assiniboine Community College	Brandon, MAN	Cougars
Augustana University College	Camrose, ALTA	Vikings

B

Beauce-Appalaches, Cégep	Ville St. Georges, PQ	Condors
Bishop's University	Lennoxville, PQ	Gaiters
Bois-de-Boulogne, Collège	Montréal, PQ	Cavaliers
Boréal, Collège	Sudbury, ONT	Vipères
Brandon University	Brandon, MAN	Bobcats
Briercrest Bible College	Caronport, SASK	Clippers
British Columbia, University of	Vancouver, BC	Thunderbirds
British Columbia Institute of Technology	Burnaby, BC	Cougars
Brock University	St. Catherines, ONT	Badgers

C

Calgary, University of	Calgary, ALTA	Dinosaurs
Cambrian College	Sudbury, ONT	Golden Shield
Camosun College	Victoria, BC	Chargers
Canadian Bible College	Regina, SASK	RISE
Canadore College	North Bay, ONT	Panthers/Kittens
Cape Breton, University College of	Sydney, NS	Capers
Capilano College	N. Vancouver, BC	Blues
Cariboo, University College of the	Kamloops, BC	Sun Demons
Carleton University	Ottawa, ONT	Ravens
Centennial College	Scarborough, ONT	Colts
Centre Université St. Louis-Maillet	Edmundson, NB	Collegians
Champlain Regional College (Lennoxville)	Lennoxville, PQ	Cougars
Champlain Regional College (St. Lambert)	St. Lambert, PQ	Cavaliers
Champlain Regional College (St. Lawrence)	Ste. Foy, PQ	Lions
Columbia Bible College	Abbotsford, BC	Concords
Concordia University College of Alberta	Edmonton, ALTA	Thunder

Junior, Senior, and Community Colleges—Canada
Alphabetic Listing by Institution

Institution Name	Location	Nickname/Mascot
Concordia University	Montreal, PQ	Stingers
Conestoga College	Kitchener, ONT	Condors
Confederation College	Thunder Bay, ONT	Thunderhawks

D

Dalhousie-Sexton Campus	Halifax, NS	Tigers
D'Alma, Cégep	Alma, PQ	Jeannois
Dawson College	Montreal, PQ	The Blues
Douglas College	New Westminster, BC	Royals
Durham College	Oshawa, ONT	Lords

E

Édouard Montpetit, Collège	Longueuil, PQ	Lynx
Erindale College (University of Toronto)	Mississauga, ONT	Warriors

F

Fairview College	Fairview, ALTA	Clippers
Fanshawe College	London, ONT	Falcons
François-Xavier-Garneau, Collège	Québec, PQ	Élans, Les
Fraser Valley, University College of the	Abbotsford, BC	Cascades

G

George Brown College	Toronto, ONT	Huskies
Georgian College	Barrie, ONT	Grizzlies
Grande Prairie Regional College	Grande Prairie, ALTA	Wolves/Cubs
Grant MacEwan College	Edmonton, ALTA	Griffins
Guelph, University of	Guelph, ONT	Gryphons

H

Haileybury School of Mines (North)	Haileybury, ONT	HSM Miners
Humber College	Etobicoke, ONT	Hawks

J

John Abbott College	Ste. Anne de Bellevue	Islanders
Jonquière, Collège de	Jonquière, PQ	Gaillards

Junior, Senior, and Community Colleges—Canada
Alphabetic Listing by Institution

Institution Name	Location	Nickname/Mascot

K

Keewatin Community College	The Pas, MAN	Cougars
Kemptville College of Agriculture Tech.	Kemptville, ONT	KATS
Keyano College	Fort McMurray, ALTA	Huskies
King's University College, The	Edmonton, ALTA	Eagles
King's College, University of	Halifax, NS	Blue Devils
Kwantlan University College	Surrey, BC	Eagles

L

La Cité Collégiale	Ottawa, ONT	Coyotes
Lakehead University	Thunder Bay, ONT	Thunderwolves
Lakeland College	Vermillion, ALTA	Rustlers
Lambton College	Sarnia, ONT	Lions
Lanaudière à Joliette, Cégep Regional	Joliette, PQ	Libellules
Langara College	Vancouver, BC	Falcons
Laurentian University	Sudbury, ONT	Voyageurs/Lady Vees
Laval, Université	Québec City, PQ	Rouge et Or
Lethbridge Community College	Lethbridge, ALTA	Kodiaks
Lethbridge, University of	Lethbridge, ALTA	Pronghorns
Limoilou, Cégep de	Québec, PQ	Titans
Loyalist College	Belleville, ONT	Lancers
Luther College	Regina, SASK	Lions

M

MacDonald College	St. Anne de Bellevue	Clansmen
Maisonneuve, Collège de	Montréal, PQ	Vikings
Malaspina University College	Nanaimo, BC	Mariners
Manitoba, University of	Winnipeg, MAN	Bisons
Marianopolis College	Montréal, PQ	Blue Demons
McGill University	Montréal, PQ	Redmen/Martlets
McMaster University	Hamilton, ONT	Marauders
Medicine Hat Community College	Medicine Hat, ALTA	Rattlers
Memorial University of Newfoundland	St. John's, NFLD	Sea-Hawks
Mohawk College	Hamilton, ONT	Mountaineers
Moncton, Université de	Moncton, NB	Aigles/Anges Bleus
Montmorency, Collège	Laval, PQ	Nomades, Les
Montréal, Université de	Montréal, PQ	Carabins
Mount Allison University	Sackville, NB	Mounties
Mount Royal College	Calgary, ALTA	Cougars
Mount St. Vincent University	Halifax, NS	Mystics

Junior, Senior, and Community Colleges—Canada
Alphabetic Listing by Institution

Institution Name	Location	Nickname/Mascot

N

New Brunswick Community College	St. John, NB	Bruins
New Brunswick, University of	Fredericton, NB	Varsity Reds
New Brunswick–St. John, University	St. John, NB	Seawolves
New Caledonia, College of	Prince George, BC	Kodiaks
Newfoundland College of Trades and Technology	St. John's, NFLD	Caribous/Tradettes
Niagara College	Welland, ONT	Knights
Nipissing University	North Bay, ONT	Lakers
North American Baptist College	Edmonton, ALTA	Crusaders
Northern Alberta Institute of Technology	Edmonton, ALTA	Ooks
Northern British Columbia, University of	Prince George, BC	Northern Timberwolves
Northern College (Kirkland Lake)	Kirkland Lake, ONT	Huskies
Northern College of Applied Arts & Technology	So. Porcupine, ONT	Raiders
Nova Scotia Agricultural College	Truro, NS	Rams
Nova Scotia, Technical University of	Halifax, NS	Engineers

O

Okanagan University College	Kelowna, BC	Lakers
Olds College	Olds, ALTA	Broncos
Ottawa, University of	Ottawa, ONT	Gee-Gees
L'Outaouais, Collège de	Hull, PQ	Griffons, Les

P

Portage College	Lac La Biche, ALTA	Voyageurs
Prairie Bible College	Three Hills, ALTA	Pilots
Prince Edward Island, University of	Charlottetown, PEI	Panthers
Providence College	Otterburne, MAN	Freemen

Q

Québec à Montréal, Université du	Montréal, PQ	Citadins
Québec à Trois-Rivières, Université du	Trois-Rivières, PQ	Patriotes
Queen's University	Kingston, ONT	Golden Gaels/Gals

R

Red Deer College	Red Deer, ALTA	Kings/Queens

Junior, Senior, and Community Colleges—Canada
Alphabetic Listing by Institution

Institution Name	Location	Nickname/Mascot
Red River Community College	Winnipeg, MAN	Rebels
Redeemer University College	Ancaster, ONT	Royals
Regina, University of	Regina, SASK	Cougars
Rockies, College of the	Cranbrook, BC	Avalanche
Royal Military College	Kingston, ONT	Paladins
Royal Military College of St. Jean	St. Jean, PQ	Remparts
Ryerson Polytechnic University	Toronto, ONT	Rams/Ewes

S

Institution Name	Location	Nickname/Mascot
St. Clair College	Windsor, ONT	Saints
St. Francis Xavier University	Antigonish, NS	X-men/X-ettes
Saint-Jean-sur-Richelieu, Cégep	Saint-Jean-sur-Richelieu, PQ	Géants
St. Lawrence College (Brockville)	Brockville, ONT	Schooners
St. Lawrence College (Cornwall)	Cornwall, ONT	Sharks
St. Lawrence College (Kingston)	Kingston, ONT	Vikings
St. Mary's University	Halifax, NS	Huskies/Belles
St. Thomas University	Fredericton, NB	Tommies
Ste. Anne de Lachine Collège	Lachine, PQ	Dragons
Ste. Anne, Université	Church Point, NS	Dragons
Sainte-Foy, Cégep de	Sainte-Foy, PQ	Dynamiques
Saskatchewan Institute of Applied Science & Technology (Kelsey Campus)	Saskatoon, SASK	Amaruks
Saskatchewan, University of	Saskatoon, SASK	Huskies
Sault College	Sault St. Marie, ONT	Cougars
Selkirk College	Castlegar, BC	Saints
Seneca College	North York, ONT	Sting
Sherbrooke, Collège de	Sherbrooke, PQ	Volontaires
Sheridan College	Oakville, ONT	Bruins
Sheridan College (Brampton)	Brampton, ONT	Bruins/Bearcats
Simon Fraser University	Burnaby, BC	Clansmen
Sir Sandford Fleming College	Peterborough, ONT	Knights
Southern Alberta Institute of Technology	Calgary, ALTA	Trojans/Helenas

T

Institution Name	Location	Nickname/Mascot
Toronto, University of	Toronto, ONT	Varsity Blues
Trent University	Peterborough, ONT	Excalibur
Trinity Western University	Langley, BC	Spartans
Trois-Rivières, Cégep de	Trois-Rivières, PQ	Diablos

Junior, Senior, and Community Colleges—Canada
Alphabetic Listing by Institution

Institution Name	Location	Nickname/Mascot
V		
Valleyfield, Cégep de	Valleyfield, PQ	Phalanges
Vanier College	Ville de St.Laurent, PQ	Cheetahs
Victoria, University of	Victoria, BC	Vikings
Victoriaville, Cégep de	Victoriaville, PQ	Vulcans
Vieux Montréal, Collège	Montréal, PQ	Spartiates
W		
Wascana Institute	Regina, SASK	Wildcats
Waterloo, University of	Waterloo, ONT	Warriors/Athenas
Western Ontario, University of	London, ONT	Mustangs
Wilfrid Laurier University	Waterloo, ONT	Golden Hawks
Windsor, University of	Windsor, ONT	Lancers
Winnipeg, University of	Winnipeg, MAN	Wesmen
Y		
York University	North York, ONT	Yeomen

Part 6

Junior, Senior, and Community Colleges

Canada

Alphabetic Listing by Nickname/Mascot

Did you know. . .

Scottdale C.C.'s Fighting Artichokes got their name, according to information supplied by Al Fisher from the sports information department, in a long struggle between students and administrators and jocks and anti-jock factions. The name was originally picked by students in a protest against the overemphasis on athletics and the lack of academic facilities. After three years of resistance, administrators (who favored the Drovers as a nickname) gave in. The Scottsdale Progress noted that this gave the mascot "more meaning than most such symbols."

Junior, Senior, and Community Colleges—Canada
Alphabetic Listing by Nickname/Mascot

Nickname/Mascot	Institution Name	Location

A

Aigles/Anges Bleus	Moncton, Université de	Moncton, NB
Amaruks	Saskatchewan Institute of Applied Science & Technology (Kelsey Campus)	Saskatoon, SASK
Avalanche	Rockies, College of the	Cranbrook, BC
Axemen	Acadia University	Wolfville, NS

B

Badgers	Brock University	St. Catherines, ONT
Bisons	Manitoba, University of	Winnipeg, MAN
Blue Demons	Marianopolis College	Montréal, PQ
Blue Devils	King's College, University of	Halifax, NS
Blues	Capilano College	N. Vancouver, BC
Bobcats	Brandon University	Brandon, MAN
Broncos	Olds College	Olds, ALTA
Bruins	New Brunswick Community College	St. John, NB
Bruins	Sheridan College	Oakville, ONT
Bruins/Bearcats	Sheridan College (Brampton)	Brampton, ONT

C

Carabins	Montréal, Université de	Montreal, PQ
Capers	Cape Breton, University College of	Sydney, NS
Caribous/Tradettes	N'foundland College of Trades & Technology	St. John's, NFLD
Cascades	Fraser Valley, University College of the	Abbotsford, BC
Cavaliers	Bois-de-Boulogne, Collège	Montréal, PQ
Cavaliers	Champlain Regional College (St. Lambert)	St. Lambert, PQ
Chargers	Camosun College	Victoria, BC
Cheetahs	Vanier College	Ville de St.Laurent, PQ
Citadins	Québec à Montréal, Université du	Montréal, PQ
Clansmen	Mac Donald College	St. Anne de Bellevue, PQ
Clansmen	Simon Fraser University	Burnaby, BC
Clippers	Briercrest Bible College	Caronport, SASK
Clippers	Fairview College	Fairview, ALTA
Collegians	Centre University St. Louis-Maillet	Edmundson, NB
Colts	Centennial College	Scarborough, ONT
Concords	Columbia Bible College	Abbotsford, BC
Condors	Beauce-Appalaches, Cégep	Ville St. Georges, PQ
Condors	Conestoga College	Kitchener, ONT
Cougars	Assiniboine Community College	Brandon, MAN

Junior, Senior, and Community Colleges—Canada
Alphabetic Listing by Nickname/Mascot

Nickname/Mascot	Institution Name	Location
Cougars	British Columbia Institute of Technology	Burnaby, BC
Cougars	Champlain Regional College (Lennoxville)	Lennoxville, PQ
Cougars	Keewatin Community College	The Pas, MAN
Cougars	Mount Royal College	Calgary, ALTA
Cougars	Regina, University of	Regina, SASK
Cougars	Sault College	S.S.Marie, ONT
Coyotes	La Cité Collégiale	Ottawa, ONT
Crusaders	North American Baptist College	Edmonton, ALTA

D

Diablos	Trois-Rivières, Cégep de	Trois-Rivières, PQ
Dinosaurs	Calgary, University of	Calgary, ALTA
Dragons	Ste.-Anne de Lachine, Collège	Lachine, PQ
Dragons	Ste. Anne, Université	Church Point, NS
Dynamiques	Sainte-Foy, Cégep de	Sainte-Foy, PQ

E

Eagles	King's University College, The	Edmonton, ALTA
Eagles	Kwantlan University College	Surrey, BC
Élans, Les	François-Xavier-Garneau, Collège	Québec, PQ
Engineers	Nova Scotia, Technology, University of	Halifax, NS
Excalibur	Trent University	Peterborough, ONT

F

Falcons	Fanshawe College	London, ONT
Falcons	Langara College	Vancouver, BC
Flames	Aldersgate College	Moosejaw, SASK
Freemen	Providence College	Otterburne, MAN

G

Gaillards	Jonquière, Collège de	Jonquière, PQ
Gaiters	Bishop's University	Lennoxville, PQ
Géants	Saint-Jean-sur-Richelieu, Cégep	S-J-S-R, PQ
Gee-Gees	Ottawa, University of	Ottawa, ONT
Golden Bears	Alberta, University of	Edmonton, ALTA
Golden Gaels/Gals	Queen's University	Kingston, ONT
Golden Hawks	Wilfrid Laurier University	Waterloo, ONT

Junior, Senior, and Community Colleges—Canada
Alphabetic Listing by Nickname/Mascot

Nickname/Mascot	Institution Name	Location
Golden Shield	Cambrian College	Sudbury, ONT
Griffins	Grant MacEwan College	Edmonton, ALTA
Griffons, Les	L'Outaouais, Collège de	Hull, PQ
Grizzlies	Georgian College	Barrie, ONT
Gryphons	Guelph, University of	Guelph, ONT

H

Hawks	Humber College	Etobicoke, ONT
HSM Miners	Haileybury School of Mines (North)	Haileybury, ONT
Huskies	George Brown College	Toronto, ONT
Huskies	Keyano College	Ft. McMurray, ALTA
Huskies	Northern College (Kirkland Lake)	Kirkland Lake, ONT
Huskies	Saskatchewan, University of	Saskatoon, SASK
Huskies	St. Mary's University	Halifax, NS

I

Idéal	André-Laurendeau, Collège	Lasalle, PQ
Indiens	Ahuntsic, Collège	Montréal, PQ
Islanders	John Abbott College	Ste.-Anne de Bellevue, PQ

J

Jeannois	D'Alma, Cégep	Alma, PQ

K

KATS	Kemptville College of Agriculture Technology	Kemptville, ONT
Kings/Queens	Red Deer College	Red Deer, ALTA
Knights	Niagara College	Welland, ONT
Knights	Sir Sandford Fleming College	Peterborough, ONT
Kodiaks	Lethbridge Community College	Lethbridge, ALTA
Kodiaks	New Caledonia, College of	Prince George, BC

L

Lakers	Nipissing University	North Bay, ONT
Lakers	Okanagan University College	Kelowna, BC
Lancers	Loyalist College	Belleville, ONT
Lancers	Windsor, University of	Windsor, ONT
Libellules	Lanaudière à Joliette, Cégep Regional	Joliette, PQ

Junior, Senior, and Community Colleges—Canada
Alphabetic Listing by Nickname/Mascot

Nickname/Mascot	Institution Name	Location
Lions	Champlain Regional College (St. Lawrence)	Ste. Foy, PQ
Lions	Lambton College	Sarnia, ONT
Lions	Luther College	Regina, SASK
Lords	Durham College	Oshawa, ONT
Lynx	Édouard Montpetit, Collège	Longueuil, PQ

M

Marauders	McMaster University	Hamilton, ONT
Mariners	Malaspina University College	Nanaimo, BC
Mountaineers	Mohawk College	Hamilton, ONT
Mounties	Mount Allison University	Sackville, NB
Mustangs	Western Ontario, University of	London, ONT
Mystics	Mount St. Vincent University	Halifax, NS

N

Nomades, Les	Montmorency, Collège	Laval, PQ
Northern Timberwolves	Northern British Columbia, University of	Prince George, BC

O

Ooks	Northern Alberta Institute of Technology	Edmonton, ALTA

P

Paladins	Royal Military College	Kingston, ONT
Panthers/Kittens	Canadore College	North Bay, ONT
Panthers	Prince Edward Island, University of	Charlottetown, PEI
Patriotes	Québec, University of (Trois-Rivières)	Trois-Rivières, PQ
Phénix	André-Grasset, Collège	Montréal, PQ
Pilots	Prairie Bible College	Three Hills, ALTA
Pronghorns	Lethbridge, University of	Lethbridge, ALTA

R

Raiders	Northern College Applied Arts & Technology	So. Porcupine, ONT
Rams	Nova Scotia Agricultural College	Truro, NS
Rams/Ewes	Ryerson Polytechnic University	Toronto, ONT
Rattlers	Medicine Hat Community College	Medicine Hat, ALTA
Ravens	Carleton University	Ottawa, ONT
Rebels	Red River Community College	Winnipeg, MAN
Redmen/Martlets	McGill University	Montreal, PQ

Junior, Senior, and Community Colleges—Canada
Alphabetic Listing by Nickname/Mascot

Nickname/Mascot	Institution Name	Location
Remparts	Royal Military College de St. Jean	St. Jean, PQ
RISE	Canadian Bible College & Seminary	Regina, SASK
Roadrunners	St. Lawrence College, St. Laurent	Cornwall, ONT
Rouge et Or	Laval University	Quebec City, PQ
Royals	Douglas College	New Westminster, BC
Royals	Redeemer University College	Ancaster, ONT
Rustlers	Lakeland College	Vermillion, ALTA

S

Saints	Selkirk College	Castlegar, BC
Saints	St. Clair College	Windsor, ONT
Schooners	St. Lawrence College (Brockville)	Brockville, ONT
Sea-Hawks	Memorial University of Newfoundland	St. John's, NFLD
Seawolves	New Brunswick—St. John, University of	St. John, NB
Sharks	St. Lawrence College (Cornwall)	Cornwall, ONT
Spartans	Trinity Western University	Langley, BC
Spartiates	Vieux Montréal, Collège	Montréal, PQ
Sting	Seneca College	North York, ONT
Stingers	Concordia University	Montreal, PQ
Sun Demons	Cariboo, University College of the	Kamloops, BC

T

The Blues	Dawson College	Montreal, PQ
Thunder	Algonquin College	Nepean, ONT
Thunder	Concordia University College of Alberta	Edmonton, ALTA
Thunderbirds	Algoma University College	Sault St. Marie, ON
Thunderbirds	British Columbia, University of	Vancouver, BC
Thunderhawks	Confederation College	Thunder Bay, ONT
Thunderwolves	Lakehead University	Thunder Bay, ONT
Tigers	Dalhousie-Sexton Campus	Halifax, NS
Titans	Limoilou, Cégep de	Québec, PQ
Tommies	St. Thomas University	Fredericton, NB
Trojans/Helenas	Southern Alberta Institute of Technology	Calgary, ALTA

V

Varsity Blues	Toronto, University of	Toronto, ONT
Varsity Reds	New Brunswick, University of	Fredericton, NB
Vikings	Augustana University College	Camrose, ALTA
Vikings	Maisonneuve, Collège de	Montréal, PQ

141

Junior, Senior, and Community Colleges—Canada
Alphabetic Listing by Nickname/Mascot

Nickname/Mascot	Institution Name	Location
Vikings	St. Lawrence College (Kingston)	Kingston, ONT
Vikings/Vikettes	Victoria, University of	Victoria, BC
Vipères	Boréal, Collège	Sudbury, ONT
Volontaires	Sherbrooke, Collège de	Sherbrooke, PQ
Voyageurs/Lady Vees	Laurentian University	Sudbury, ONT
Voyageurs	Portage College	Lac La Biche, ALTA
Vulcans	Victoriaville, Cégep de	Victoriaville, PQ

W

Nickname/Mascot	Institution Name	Location
Warriors	Erindale College (University of Toronto)	Mississauga, ONT
Warriors/Athenas	Waterloo, University of	Waterloo, ONT
Wesmen	Winnipeg, University of	Winnipeg, MAN
Wildcats	Wascana Institute	Regina, SASK
Wolves/Cubs	Grande Prairie Regional College	Grande Prairie, ALTA

X

Nickname/Mascot	Institution Name	Location
X-men/X-ettes	St. Francis Xavier University	Antigonish, NS

Y

Nickname/Mascot	Institution Name	Location
Yeomen	York University	North York, ONT

If you enjoyed this book, why not order one for a friend?
Quantity Discounts Available

Order Blank

- **A Must for Every Sports Bar**
- **Great Ice Breaker for any Sports Party**
- **Perfect Gift for Every Sports Enthusiast**
- **Keep One in the Glove Compartment of Your Car**

Name _____

Address _____

City _____ State ____ Zip _____

Phone _____ Fax _____

E-Mail Address _____

Comments _____

_____

_____

_____

_____ copies @ $19.95 ea. = _____

7% Sales Tax (Florida residents) _____

Total _____

Plus Shipping and Handling
$3.50 for the first book
$1.50 for each additional copy _____

Grand Total _____

Make Check Payable to:

Raja and Associates

Mail to:

Raja and Associates
16807 Harrierridge Pl.
Lithia, FL 33547

Watch for the next edition of
The Handbook of
Mascots & Nicknames
which will include Puerto Rician
colleges and institutions of higher learning